From Knock Down to Comeback:

How I Used My Personal Tragedy to Find My Purpose and Passion

7-3-2020

Juliet Lamin

Acknowledgements

I would like to thank everyone whose unwavering love and support throughout my dark years made it possible to write this book.

I will always thank God for you, Michael Lee, my husband and encourager. I don't know how I would have coped without your love and support.

My stepchildren, Daniel, Kieran and Sarah—thank you for your acceptance, particularly on those hard Mothers' and Christmas Days.

My warmest gratitude to my publisher and publishing consultant Sidney Sanni and his fantastic team. Your insight and advise proved invaluable to me.

I'm profoundly grateful to my spiritual parents and mentors, whose love, coaching and mentoring over the years made me the stronger, wiser and better person I am today.

A massive thank you goes to the Bexleyheath Academy staff and pupils for their continued love towards me. Thank you for granting me the privilege to freely visit the school whenever I want to turn up and sit in Philip's memorial garden.

Thanks to all my friends from the Bexley community for standing with me. I am so pleased to live in one of the best boroughs in the country.

My deep appreciation goes to my family for their love, prayers and support. I couldn't have asked to be born into a better family.

Thank you, Mark Adams, for sharing two compelling stories with my readers and me.

Len and Yvonne Randal and the entire family, thanks for adopting me into your family. I love you guys with all my heart.

To my faith families: BCLC, BBC, VBCI and FCI, for all your support at different times of my journey.

What can I say about every young person who has passed through PL9? You have all been amazing. Thank you for all the love and continuous messages of encouragement.

Finally, a very special thank you goes to my best friends who stuck to me like glue when the crowds finally disappeared. To the ones who were there in all of my darkest, most painful, loneliest and most vulnerable moments. My rocks who stuck it out with me and gave me strength through these words from my Saviour:

> '[Juliet, Juliet], Satan has asked to sift each of you like wheat. But I have pleaded in prayer for you, [Juliet], that your faith should not fail. So when you have repented and turned to me again, strengthen your brothers.' (Luke 22:31 NLT)

Table of Contents

Juliet and Philip

The beginning of my story

The story that led me to write this book started on the 21st of December 2011, at exactly 11 pm.

I was at home, in my bedroom, getting ready for bed after a long day at work. Philip, my fourteen-year-old son and only child, was somewhere in the house. As it was the start of his Christmas holidays, he had asked to stay up late to play his football game on the Xbox. During term time I was always quite strict about his bedtime routine. But I agreed to his persuasive arguments to play a little longer that evening since, during the previous term, he had done his homework consistently and kept to his routines without too much coaxing from me.

As the time edged towards 11 pm, there was a knock at the door and my son popped his head through my bedroom door to ask if he should go downstairs and open the door. At first, I said no, as I wasn't expecting anyone at that time of the night. However, the person at the door continued knocking, so Philip went off to find out who it was. I stayed behind to put on my robe before following him down-stairs. Philip peered through the key hole, but couldn't make out who was outside. He opened the door cautiously, and to my sur-prise, our visitor was Joe Conway (not his real name), a young boy who used to live in our neighbourhood with his parents, but had recently moved elsewhere.

We opened the door for him to come in, and he entered, looking rather anxious and ner-vous. Philip was just happy to see his friend and took him straight into the lounge to join him on the Xbox; I was more suspicious about why a fourteen-year-old boy had been knock-ing persistently at my door so late at night.

'Joe, what on earth are you doing out so late?' I asked. My suspicion must have leaked through my voice, because he frowned.

'Good evening, Auntie.' He looked at me, his brow still furrowed. I was not his biological aunt, but as a mark of respect, it is traditional for African people to refer to their elders as 'Auntie' and 'Uncle'. 'I was just passing by and decided to stop by and say hello to you and Philip.'

I decided to give him the benefit of the doubt. 'It's a little late for you to be wandering around, Joe. Would you like to spend the night?'

His face brightened. 'Yes, Auntie.'

He declined my offer of some food with a brief, 'I'm not hungry,' before turning his attention to his game with Philip. I left them in the living room engaging in youthful banter and went upstairs to get the guest room ready for him, since Philip would never share his bedroom with anyone. I was making the bed when it suddenly occurred to me to call his mother and find out exactly why her child was out so late, so I hurried to get my phone.

The phone rang twice before she picked it up. I got straight to the point. 'Charlene (not her real name, either), Joe is here.'

'Juliet? Oh, thank goodness!' She said, with a heavy sigh of relief, but quickly went on to tell me all hell was breaking loose at her house. There were several police officers in her home, numerous police cars outside and a few helicopters buzzing overhead, all of them searching for her son. She was distressed, I was shocked and the conversation ended abruptly as I told her I would call back shortly because I needed to speak to her son.

I went downstairs immediately. 'Philip, go to your room. I need to talk to Joe in private.' From the tone of my voice, my son must have sensed that there was a problem. He immediately switched the game off and left the room.

I sat down and faced Joe. 'Right, young man. I would like a better explanation for you turning up at my house this late in the night. And before you start, you should know that I spoke to your mother, and I know about the large number of police officers at your house.' My initially welcoming tone was gone, and judging by the way he immediately straightened his posture, Joe knew it.

Shoulders slumped, he bowed his head dramatically and launched into explaining the events that led him to my house. In essence, he had been hanging out with a few of his friends around the 'ends'—layman's terms for his neighbourhood—when some youths walked up and started behaving aggressively.

'We told them to get lost because we didn't want any trouble,' he said, his eyes pleading with me to believe his story, 'but one of the boys punched my friend on the nose. That's why the fight started, Auntie. It wasn't our fault.'

I was still trying to process what Joe was telling me when he added that one of the boys who had caused the trouble then deliberately cut himself with a knife, dialled 999, and told the police that someone had just stabbed him!

'We knew the police would soon arrive and there would be even more trouble, so we scattered in separate directions, and I ended up close to your house.'

I took a breath to absorb what I had been told. 'You're not going to escape by running away from the police, Joe. And it is not a good idea to try to, especially as they are already at your house looking for you.'

'Auntie, what do you want me to do?' He looked thoroughly confused. 'I ran away in the first place because I thought that was the right thing at the time.'

I advised him to turn himself over to the police, and offered to accompany him to the station so he could explain what had happened. He agreed, so I called his mum back to explain the situation and my advice to her son.

Charlene agreed that it was the right thing to do, so I immediately phoned the police, gave them my details and informed them Joe Conway was coming down to the station to turn himself in, and that I would be acting as an appropriate adult. The lady in the Police Control Room asked several questions, noted down all the information and agreed to my suggestion. She asked how long it would take us to arrive.

'I was already in bed when Joe arrived, so I'll need to change out of my pyjamas, but we should be there shortly.'

'Okay, we'll be expecting you,' she said, and hung up.

A quick change of clothes later, I was waiting for Joe's father to pick us up and drive us to the police station when, to my surprise, I spotted two policemen walking towards my house.

I met them outside, greeted them politely and explained that I was waiting for a lift to the station. I did this to protect my son who didn't know what was going on. I had not yet explained the reason for Joe's visit.

To my utter amazement, the male officer shouted in my face, 'You don't tell the police what to do, we tell you what to do!'

I was horrified. I had been a Youth worker for about 12 years and worked with multiple agencies including the police. At work, we often called them in to help with challenging situations and we always worked together.

They were usually polite and understanding. However, on this particular day, this officer was rude and completely unprofessional. He barged past me into the house and demanded that I produce Joe immediately.

As a result of his actions, the situation quickly escalated. The boys were in Philip's bedroom, so I called Joe to come down quickly because the police had arrived. As he came down, the police officer lunged past me, grabbed him and pulled him headfirst down the stairs. This caused him to fall on top of the police officer who began punching him repeatedly in the groin. Joe cried out for my help as he was in a lot of pain.

I did not really know what to do, but I was definitely worried about the level of violence, so I asked Philip to record it on his mobile phone, which he did from the top of the stairs. It later turned out to be a very important record of what went on that night.

When the officer realised he was being recorded, he took out his pepper spray and sprayed it in Philip's direction.

'Mum,

I can't see! Mum, I can't breathe!' Philip was screaming and Joe was still crying out for help. I was so scared. It was like being in a horror movie, except this was taking place in my own house.

Before I knew what was happening, Joe had been taken off in a police van with his father, who had arrived during the commotion. Over twenty police officers were now in my house, eight of them in my living room where they had placed me in handcuffs, and approximately seven in my hallway where they handcuffed Philip. He kept calling for me, but they wouldn't let us be together. The other officers ransacked and turned our bedrooms upside down. I kept asking why they were doing this to me as I had done the right thing, but no one would give me a straightforward answer. Eventually, Philip and I were hauled off to the police station in separate vehicles. All because one police officer misunderstood the situation and refused to co-operate.

We were detained from the night of the 21st until the 23rd of December when we appeared in court. However, the case could not be completed on that day and was adjourned for a second hearing. It was then further postponed.

During this period, Philip was in the middle of his mock exams. I called the school to explain the situation and asked if they could support him by writing a character reference. The Head of Year at that time agreed, but she later stopped taking my calls. My pastor wrote to those in charge of the police case, asking them to consider dropping it since I acted with good intent. Unfortunately, nobody wanted to get involved. Even my lawyer made it very clear that we might not win because, by law, the government is duty bound to protect the police. I asked her to represent us regardless. I had done nothing wrong, and if we were to suffer or go to prison for doing the right thing, so be it.

On the 19th of April 2012, we went for our final hearing. To support my family, a group of my friends fasted and prayed. Several pastors and leaders in our church were also praying for us, and my senior pastor at the time accompanied us to court.

The police told their version of the event and my son and I did the same. After the judge listened to our story and viewed the video Philip had recorded on his phone, he stated that I was a woman of integrity. He believed I had acted reasonably and responsibly in taking this young man into my house, offering him food to eat and a bed for the night, checking with his mother and then calling the police to make them aware of Joe's whereabouts.

To God's glory, we were fully vindicated. The judge went on to say the police were heavy-handed in the way they handled the matter.

After the court hearing concluded, Philip and I developed a complete lack of trust in the police. My feelings of resentment towards them increased daily. I also became very worried about how my son was coping after the negative experience of the police pushing both of us around in our own home, and then locking us up in a police cell for two days for no just cause. I must have asked Philip how he was feeling no fewer than twenty times, and his response was always the same:

'I'm alright, Mum, but I will never trust the police again for what they did to us in our own home.'

P.U.S.H
(Pray until something happens)

As I began to develop an intense aversion towards the police and my son's distrust towards them kept growing, I realised I had to do something very radical, and decided to take my prayer life to a new level.

I fasted and prayed every day for almost three months, asking God to give us the grace to forgive the police. During this period, several friends advised me to sue for compensation, which I thought was a brilliant idea. Before taking action, however, I decided to seek the counsel of my pastor and spiritual mentor. He suggested that I forgive the police and let God, who had vindicated me, take care of my compensation. To be honest, it wasn't really what I wanted to hear but I chose to obey his sound advice and voice of wisdom.

During this period, while I prayed and fasted, God was working behind the scenes. In July, I was promoted at work at a time when I had been concerned about losing my job following my involvement with the police. Fulham football club also scouted my son to play professionally for the under-16s. This led to a great sense of joy in our family.

As I received the grace to do so, I began to think positive thoughts towards the police. God not only placed a special compassion in my heart for them, He opened the eyes of my heart to help me see the police as vulnerable human beings. They were just like me—susceptible to making mistakes under pressure and deserved the same forgiveness I would expect from God.

One day during my prayer time, I spent a considerable number of hours crying uncontrollably for the police force. I had never experienced anything of this sort before. I then heard a clear voice telling me not to go a day without praying for them. I took this as an assignment and began praying every day, and soon found myself calling out random names of people I somehow knew were in the police force. On one occasion, I was inspired to pray for John, Peter, James, Matthew and Tony, and I knew they all worked for the police. I prayed God's blessings on their homes and families, asking God to help them as they went about their work, to grant them wisdom and understanding in difficult situations, particularly in any situation similar to ours.

I also prayed that God would forgive them for what they had done to my family and remove all negative memories from our minds. Sometimes I would go to my local police station and prayer walk around the building. I do this even today, but more about that later.

We had a brilliant Christmas in 2012, which we enjoyed tremendously as we began to let go of the stressful year that was 2011.

Good news all the way!

Like I said, earlier in 2012, I was promoted at work when I had thought I would be dismissed. Instead of a criminal record, I was rewarded with a promotion.

In the same year around June or July, I received a phone call from Philip's school, from the manager of an under-16s professional football club. He stated that he had been watching Philip play, that he was an amazing footballer with an exceptional character, and they were interested in scouting him to play for their under-16s.

I remained calm while he was talking to me, and didn't let him know how excited I was. As soon as I hung up, I screamed and danced around the house for a while. Then I went to get dinner ready for my son, thinking about how I would break the good news to him when he came back. Not much later, Philip burst through the door.

'Mum, mum, did anybody call you?'

'Yes, I had a call from your school.' I said, as calmly as I had been during the phone call.

'What did he say, WHAT DID HE SAY?!'

I decided to bring the suspense to an end and told him what the manager said. He grabbed me into a tight hug and we cried. Our joy was indescribable.

After that, Philip became even more dedicated to his football career, waking up to practice each day before school. One morning, he suddenly said,

'You need to increase my dinner money, Mum.'

'And why should I do that?'

'Because you are looking at a professional footballer, now, and my tastes and stomach have become expensive.'

On another occasion, he asked me to create an IOU card, and every now and again, he would ask me to put some money on it as a loan. The first time he asked me for the card, I laughed.

'What on earth do you need an IOU card for?'

'Well, I will owe you a mansion and a Lamborghini once I start earning a footballer's salary. There is one condition, though....'

'And that is...?'

'That you remain single so that you can stay at home and look after my children!'

We would often laugh about this, but I became prouder of him every day. I watched my son become incredibly mature and overly loving and caring toward me. Every day, when he returned from school, he would call for me to come downstairs as soon as he entered the house. He would grab hold of my hand and usher me into the lounge; wrap his arms around me and ask me to stand with him for five minutes. Philip would then start praising me, telling me how privileged he was to have me as his mum and that he had seen how I had sacrificed a multitude of things to get him to where he was. He did this every day.

Another miracle

In the same summer of 2012, I experienced another miracle. One beautiful Wednesday afternoon, I received a phone call from Margaret (not her real name), a lady friend who attended the Monday prayer group I conducted.

'Juliet, what are you doing later this evening?'

'I'm free tonight.' I said. 'What did you have in mind?'

'It's no big deal, but could I pop in to see you around seven?'

I was mildly curious but saw no reason to disagree, so we arranged for her to drop in later. She arrived at 7.15pm, entered the lounge and asked me to sit down.

She sat adjacent from me on the couch.

'I need to tell you something, Juliet, but you must promise not to reject what I want to offer you.'

'Margaret, I'm not going to make any promises until I hear what you have to say,' I told her, my curiosity growing by the second.

Margaret began to tell me *strange* stories. She had experienced sleepless nights over the past three days during which the Lord had asked her to give me her Mercedes Benz.

'What for?' I asked, astounded.

'That's what I got from my dream, Juliet.' She said.

'Are you sure you heard properly, Margaret?'

She replied without hesitation. 'Yes,'

I was shocked. Margaret had two young children, aged five and three. 'How are you going to get the children to school?'

Her reply dumbfounded me. 'Public transport.'

I repeated my question, and she gave the same answer.

'With your children? To school?'

'Yes.'

'Are you certain?' I was baffled as to why God would want to make her life difficult in order to make mine comfortable, particularly as I didn't need a car at the time. Even my son was fifteen-years-old and could go to school by himself.

'This was the reason I asked you to brace yourself when I arrived, Juliet.' She continued. 'Please don't deny me my blessing.'

At that point, it felt like she had tied my hands. I couldn't very well deprive her of the reward she could expect for obeying God's instruction. 'Alright, Margaret,' I said. 'If that is how you feel, I'll simply say "thank you".'

She took me outside and showed me round the beautiful car, painstakingly telling me everything I needed to know about it. We drove around my street before she tearfully handed me the car keys, called for a cab and left.

I went back to my lounge, dropped to my knees and had a private discussion with God. 'Why did You have to do that, Lord? Why would You take a car from someone who needs it and give it to me when I don't have any use for it?'

I then began to pray in earnest for Margaret. 'Lord, for the pain this young mother has to go through in order to obey Your voice, I pray you will send her blessings that far exceed the owning of cars. Favour her in every department of her life, Lord. Put her in the position to experience '...*eyes have not seen, nor have ears heard, neither have entered into the heart of men...*'[1] miracles that are beyond her wildest imagination. Enlarge her territory, grant every desire of her heart and protect her children.'

After I finished praying for her, I went to prepare Philip's dinner. I waited until we were sitting at the dining table before I told him about my gift.

'Whattttt? What did you say, Mum?' He didn't believe me until I took out the car keys and showed him the log book, which was already in my name. Suddenly, he grabbed his Bible and went straight to his bedroom.

I hurried after him and put my ear to the door to hear what was happening. Philip was crying. I started crying, too. After a while, he came back downstairs and held me again.

'Mum, God sure does know how to compensate.' He said. 'I now know why you are so in love with him. Thank you for introducing him to me at an early age.'

This was the end of our miracle in 2012.

---

1   1 Corinthians 2:9

There was one further miracle in 2012, where I came to meet Mike, the man who would become my husband, but that deserves a book in its own right.

My darkest days

2013

The month of February started like any other month, with me going to work and Philip attending school and football training.

On the 5th, he came to my room and asked for his dinner money, which I gave to him just like every other morning.

'Can I have some more?' He asked.

'I've put enough money in your bank account, Philip,' I told him, 'but it is not for spending carelessly. Use it only when necessary.'

He left that morning and said goodbye to me as usual. When he left the house, he shouted back through the window. 'Bye, Mum!'

'Goodbye,' I replied, 'God bless you, Son.'

When I woke up that day, for some reason, I had an overwhelming urge to spring clean my house. I started with Philip's room, then cleaned the whole house. Afterwards, a friend of mine came over at noon and left at 2.20pm to pick up her kids from the school near my house. As soon as she left, I went to the kitchen to get dinner ready because that would be the first thing Philip asked for when he arrived.

While I was in the kitchen, the phone rang. It was Philip's best friend, Miljan, asking me to make my way to the school. He explained that my son had scored a goal during a football game, and as his friends were cheering him on, he went in for another tackle and suddenly collapsed.

I had received many phone calls from Miljan, but this time he sounded very different, he was crying. I realised the situation was severe.

'Is everything okay?' I was prompted to ask him. 'Is Philip still breathing?'

His reply was not convincing, so I told him I was on my way and hung up. I immediately dropped to my knees and prayed that God would take control of whatever was going on. Then I left for the school. I must have been about ten minutes away when I received another phone call, this time from a teacher, asking me to go straight to the hospital the ambulance had transferred him to where they had the equipment to attend to him. I changed direction and drove to the hospital.

On my way there, I called my son's dad, my immediate family, my church family and my pastor. I explained the situation and asked them to pray. On arriving at the hospital, I was ushered into a room where my son was lying on a stretcher. He had tubes all over his body, and about seven doctors were trying to revive him. The scene was too much for me to handle, so I asked the nurses if they could give me a private room, which they did. I went in, knelt down and started praying to God to save my son. After half an hour or so, I went back in. Philip was still unresponsive. The doctors told me they were going to cease their attempts to resuscitate him, as there was nothing more they could do.

I pleaded with them not to stop, but to continue for another half hour. They carried on, and I went back in thirty minutes later, but there was still no response.

My son was pronounced dead right in front of me.

I could not believe it. He was as healthy as any normal child could be, and had shown no sign of illness. He was a fit child who never joked around with his food. I rang Mike in Dorset and asked him to promise me that Philip was going to be okay. I must have sounded confused because he asked me to pass the phone to the nurse. She told him the same thing—Philip had passed away.

After hearing this again, I must have lost my mind because I ran out of the hospital straight onto the main road, lay down and hoped a car would run me over and take my life. I wanted to join my son. Fortunately, several people ran after me, stopped the oncoming vehicles and took me back to the hospital where my son's dead body was lying. By this time the news of his death had been leaked through social media. More than a hundred of his friends from school, my family, and friends joined me at the hospital. We did all we could, praying and begging God to bring Philip back, to no avail.

It took Mike 2½ hours to drive from Dorset to the hospital. As he took me into his arms, I kept pleading with him to bring my son back. We were in the hospital for over five hours, after which I was taken home.

By the time I arrived, my street was packed with people from the local community. My house was full of people I knew and didn't know; who all came to show their concern and sympathy. Due to the trauma of the day, I have very little recollection of that night, but I remember the doorbell ringing until late and a constant stream of well-wishers praying with me until the early hours.

Oh God, Let this be a dream!

I woke up the next morning, wondering whether it had simply been a nightmare, but as I came down and saw my friends who had kept a vigil going all night, I realised the nightmare was, in fact, reality.

For some reason, even though I was feeling my own pain, I had an overwhelming sense of care and duty towards Philip's friends and teachers and felt a tremendous need to visit the school that day. My pastor contacted the school and was advised that the main hall had been set aside as a memorial area where the students could gather and share their grief. At about 11am, my pastor and I, along with about ten close friends, made our way to the school. We were met by the headmaster who shook our hands and offered his condolences. At the time, I recall thinking what a huge responsibility this new head teacher had on his shoulders; he had only been at the school a few weeks and he now had to deal with the death of a student, grieving students and staff, as well as having a school to run. I asked him how he was and *how he was coping*, a phrase he later told me has stuck with him. For the first time, I also met Philip's Head of

Year who only had taken on the role during a last minute change at the beginning of that school year.

We were ushered into the main school hall where there were tables of floral and football tributes, cards and drawings that the students had brought in as a memorial to Philip. I was feeling so much of my own pain as I took in all the tributes and a huge projected photo of Philip across the front of the hall, but as I looked around at all the young people there, the pain and hurt they were clearly going through helped me compose myself and be strong for them.

I asked Philip's Head of Year to take us to the place where he collapsed. It was a cold walk through sleety rainfall on that February morning, as we crossed the fields to the small *AstroTurf* pitches where the boys had been playing. Emotion overwhelmed me as I lay down on the spot where Philip had collapsed, trying in some way to get a connection with him again.

This school and the Bexley community will never be the same, I recall whispering. I made a vow to spend the rest of my life exposing whatever had killed my son and campaigning to stop it happening again and leaving another mother without her child.

Leaving the school, we made our way to the mortuary to see Philip. A few of his close friends wanted to come along, and though some of the adults thought it might be too emotional and stressful for them, I agreed because I felt it would help us all start the grieving process of coming to terms with his death. The visit was very uplifting; we sang and prayed around his body which looked so peaceful, as though he was only asleep and enjoying the moment.

The next few days were a blur to me. There was so much to sort out, and I still had a constant flow of friends and well-wishers coming to my house who would stay and cook even when I was out.

My pastor and Mike, usually the only white people in the huge crowd of well-wishers in my home, didn't understand the black tradition of friends and family demonstrating their support by being around day and night. They felt I should be allowed to rest and cope with grieving on my own. One evening, my pastor stood up at about 10pm and asked everyone to give me some peace and space. Out of respect, about half of the guests got up and said their farewells, but no sooner had they left than the doorbell rang and even more friends and family poured in. In my grieving state, I chuckled quietly as my Pastor and Mike gave each other resigned looks, knowing they would have no influence over the numbers or how long people were going to stay.

Philip had an old pet rabbit. It usually stayed indoors, enjoying the warmth of the house, and had its sleeping area in a corner of the living room. One of my friends thought the constant stream of visitors would be too stressful for it, so kindly offered to look after it. It is often said that animals are aware of changes in the house. The rabbit passed away exactly one week after Philip. While my friend was concerned that I would be upset about losing the pet, it gave me a bit of comfort to think that Philip had been reunited with his pet rabbit.

I, however, had bigger things that were causing me extreme stress and anxiety. Mike, who had taken time off work to help me organise matters, was driving through Welling to pick up some medication from my doctor when he had a sudden urge to stop at the Co-operative funeralcare store. He went in and explained the situation. The lady behind the desk was aware of Philip's passing as it had been widely publicised in the local and national newspapers. She made a few phone calls and advised that they would carry out Philip's funeral arrangements free of charge, except for the local council's costs. However, they were unable to plan the funeral until the coroner released Philip's body.

This process was one of the most difficult I have ever, and hopefully, will ever have to go through in my life. Philip had died suddenly, so I had to attend the coroner's office to find out how he died. For future medical research, they wanted to carry out investigations on Philip's heart and internal organs, which I knew meant operating on my precious son. If I consented to their removing all the organs they wanted in one go, they could release Philip's body back to me quickly, but the process would be much longer if they were to take small samples. I could not bring myself to let them harvest major parts of Philip's body, so I made the painful decision to wait. We made appointments to visit the coroner during which we were allowed to observe Philip behind a glass screen.

While he was just lying there peacefully, my faith believed that by God's supernatural intervention and our prayers, he could miraculously be brought back to life, so having to give my permission to remove parts of his body caused me the most awful pain any mother could go through. This was compounded by the fact that I had to wait until the coroner obtained the medical results before they would release my son's body to me, so I could continue with his funeral arrangements.

My son passed away on the 5th of February 2013 and I was finally able to lay him to rest on the 8th of March. I can say without any doubt that this was the worst month of the worst year of my life.

Philip is finally laid to rest

I woke up on the 8th of March 2013, full of fear and apprehension, still praying that some miracle would wake my son up and bring him back to me. I lay on my bedroom floor for two hours and prayed for strength and guidance. It was during this prayer time that I felt my body being taken over by the Holy Spirit, and a different kind of peace that I hadn't experienced before filled me. I showered, dressed and made my way to the church. When I arrived, I was greeted by almost a thousand friends, family, and well-wishers. The inner peace I had received during prayer helped me be strong for the young people gathered to say goodbye to their friend.

That day I felt like a tiny stick in the midst of a turbulent sea, being carried along by the wave of emotion. I knew events were totally out of my hands. I have been told I was a source of strength and inspiration to other people there, but the only person steering my ship that day was the Lord, by the power of his Holy Spirit in me.

There were so many people standing on the stage paying tribute to Philip; his teachers, his friends, his headmaster, his football coach and his pastors.

One of the tributes I clearly recollect was by the Bishop of a church I am affiliated with, in which he said, 'life is not about how long we live on this earth, but what we achieve while we are here. Some people live a long life and don't achieve very much and some people live a short life, yet their legacy lives on forever.'

I remember thinking to myself at the time that I would make sure Philip's legacy lives on forever. I also think those words encouraged me to stand up in front of everyone and pay my own personal tribute to Philip. It was not something I had rehearsed or even planned, but I felt the urge to pay tribute to my son, and I was given the grace and strength by

God to deliver my message in front of everyone without breaking down in tears or giving in to my emotions.

His close friends showed great fortitude as they raised my son's coffin onto their shoulders and carried him out to the hearse.

It was a cold, wet day, but that did not stop over 800 people following the hearse on foot and walking nearly a mile in the rain to the cemetery. It is African tradition that a mother should not attend the burial of her child. Even on the day, I was advised not to go, but I refused. I wasn't going to allow tradition to stop me from saying my final farewell to my son. So, I stood there in the rain with everyone else, praising and worshipping God. I remember starting the song and being joined by everyone, with the words:

> *My soul magnify the Lord and my spirit praise his name, for death could not hold him captive, and even in the grave, Jesus is Lord.*

The coffin was lowered into the ground, and another point in the closure of my grieving was behind me.

Philip, my son, had been laid to rest.

The post-mortem

One morning several months later, a large envelope dropped onto my doormat. Thinking it was a regular bill, I opened it and started to read what turned out to be the gruesome details of the post mortem. It was shockingly graphic and I felt physically and emotionally sick as the whole episode came back to me. Thankfully, Mike, who was with me at the time, took the document away and kept it at his house to shield me from the pain.

In summary, the post mortem results showed that my son had suffered a sudden cardiac arrest (SCA).

How? Why? When did he become sick?

I started researching this illness because I'd never heard about it before. I discovered that it was prevalent, but there was very little public awareness of it. Apparently, twelve fit and healthy young people die every week in the UK alone as a result of this cardiac illness.

Life has to go on!

The funeral and burial gave me some closure, but it also brought me down to earth with a huge bump. The daily vigil of friends, family and well-wishers from the day Philip died to his funeral eventually disappeared and I was left to deal with life without Philip.

Day to day things that I would normally easily deal with became massive tasks. I was prescribed strong doses of anti-depressants to calm me down and help me sleep, but they did not work. I remember having to phone the Child Benefit and Child Tax Credit agencies to let them know Philip had passed away. Their sympathy did not prevent them from immediately stopping the payments.

My grief prevented me from coping and I was in no position to return to my career in social care. I had been responsible for counselling people with serious social problems involving drugs, alcohol and domestic violence.

That job was something I was in no state of mind to return to.

I did receive some financial help from the government, but without the income I was used to, I quickly went into arrears with my bills and mortgage payments. The institutions were sympathetic to my situation, but they needed guarantees that they would be paid. I was in no fit state to give such assurances and can only thank God that Mike was able to support me emotionally and financially at this time. Without his help with paying my mortgage (in addition to his own), I would have lost my house. As well as working full time, he frequently travelled between Dorset and Kent to support and help me recover.

Looking back, I can now see why, the first time they met, Philip told me to hang on to Mike; that he would be good for me, although I'm certain Philip had his own agenda at the time. He knew Mike would take his place in giving me English lessons and probably felt he would get new pairs of trainers as part of the deal.

Philip's Friends

After Philip's burial, it was obvious that his friends were in a complete state of confusion. Their grieving was really intense as they missed him terribly. After school, they would come straight to my house where we would cook, eat, laugh and cry all at the same time. This carried on every day, and their numbers increased each week. I suddenly went from being a mother of one son to becoming a mother to more than 200 children on a week-ly basis.

One day, I was in the shower when I felt a hand on my shoulder. The atmosphere was extremely peaceful, and I heard a clear voice say to me, 'Mum, would you please look after my friends?'

I broke down in tears and said yes. I made a vow, through my pain and grieving, that I would dedicate the rest of my life to honouring that voice.

On the 5th of June 2013, about a month or so after I made that vow, and exactly five months after Philip's death, another young person in his school year died suddenly. The tragic irony of it all was that some of my son's friends were at his graveside when they got the news that the young girl had died. She was only 15. In shock, some of them came straight to my house. They were deeply upset, and they began questioning me about God and faith. A number of them with Christian backgrounds and parents started doubting God's existence. They came to their own conclusion that very day, that there can't be a God. After all, if there was a God, how could he possibly allow a 16-year-old and a 15-year-old from the same school, both of whom had so much to live for, to die within five months?

To be honest, due to my own vulnerability at the time, I almost found myself agreeing with every doubt around me. I did not know how to make sense of the questions, especially to these teenagers. I found myself questioning God.

What was he up to in allowing everything that was happening?

Why let my only child die at 16, and then confuse the young people further by taking another one of their school mates?

As awesome and mighty as He is, couldn't He have at least saved my only child who was just 16 years old?

I reminded God of all the good works I had done for Him and in His name; the countless hours and sleepless nights I had spent in prayer, feeding the homeless, visiting the sick in hospital, encouraging single mothers and even visiting some of their children in prison.

To my shame, after I reminded God of all of my good works, He reminded me of the sacrifice of His Son; of the thirty-three and a half years that His only Son was absent from heaven. How Jesus suffered disgrace, shame, mockery, humiliation and brutality at the hands of cruel men. God reminded me of the barbarity of the cross on which His Son was crucified. All these and more happened so He and I could be reconciled. On hearing His side of the story I broke down in shame and wept.

I knew then that I could never win an argument with God and decided to do what Jesus did in Luke 22:41-43(NLT):

> *He walked away about a stone's throw, and knelt down and prayed, 'Father, if you are willing, please take this cup of suffering away from me. Yet I want your will to be done, not mine.' Then an angel from heaven appeared and strengthened him.*

After that day, as I surrendered to and co-operated with God, events began to unfold in ways I cannot explain.

The number of Philip's friends visiting my house on a weekly basis practically doubled. They came from all over the community. I had never set eyes on majority of them, but when I saw their pain and the stress they were going through (taking their GCSE's while grieving the loss of Philip and Jane), I decided to put my own sorrow on the back burner and look after them, knowing how much they trusted and wanted to be around me. Some of them would occasionally arrive at my house with extra clothing to sleep over, staying up very late to revise for their exams.

We would cook Jollof rice and chicken, a very popular meal among the boys, or we would order pizza. They would chat about Philip, sometimes wearing his clothes or lying in his bed in an attempt to feel his presence. Seeing them like this was very emotional for me. I would often leave them, go to the toilet and cry before returning to join them.

I turned pain into a project

It got to a point when I could no longer handle the growing numbers in my house. They increased by the week, so I decided to move them out of my house to a public venue. I approached my local *Nando's* and asked for a space to set up a youth forum. They immediately gave me their upper room, which takes about 25 to 30 people and we started meeting there weekly. I also asked my local church for financial support so I could provide them with food. My pastor and church leaders agreed to sponsor me on a monthly basis. So, working with Emmanuel, Philip's cousin and childhood friend, I started a forum called PL9, using Philip's initials, and the number nine, which was his football jersey number.

Initially, the forum was just to help my son's school friends through the grieving process while taking their GCSE's, but as time went on, news spread to neighbouring schools and young people from about 17 different schools began to show up. PL9 became somewhere not only to grieve positively but to talk freely about the many issues affecting their lives.

Building bridges between young people and the police

Every week, as I listened to them discuss various topics, it became apparent that the most pressing problem among the ethnic minority youth is the frequency with which the police used their Stop and Search powers, and that it had resulted in complete fear and distrust of the police.

Even the gentlest black youth in the room became visibly upset and passionate, and would talk non-stop once they started this discussion. This carried on each week. Having gone through a negative experience with my son and the police, I understood where the boys were coming from, and why they felt this way.

After hearing the same concerns for several weeks, I decided to help the youngsters. I recognised that if something drastic were not done, the nation would breed a generation who would grow up hating the police because of unpleasant encounters and experiences that would be recounted to their own children, resulting in a similar hatred of the police and creating an unending cycle of negativity.

My pastor, the borough police chaplain, introduced me to our borough police commander who had heard about my work in the community and wanted to meet me. When my pastor spoke to him, it was actually divine timing and we arranged a meeting. Some of the boys and I went to his office where we exchanged views in a really positive and productive way. He showed genuine concern as the young people poured their hearts out to him. We then made another appointment for him to attend our forum to meet the others.

On the day of his visit, there were about 40 charged up and passionate young people in the room, ready to vent all their resentment and frustration over their continuous negative experiences with the police. I advised the borough commander to prepare to be challenged. I also encouraged the youth to be constructive if they wanted to be listened to, and not to just talk with misguided anger. I told them to channel their wrath correctly in order to bring about a positive solution to the issues at hand.

PL9

However, when the borough commander arrived, he was friendly, charismatic and well prepared. The previously angry teens became so nice and humble, I will forever be proud of them. He introduced himself, sat down among the kids and set about defusing the 'them' and 'us' situation by creating a friendly environment that fostered trust and mutual respect. His soothing manner caused the youths to open up to him about their experiences. He took all their comments on board, and, quite surprisingly, humbled himself and apologised where he accepted that the police had gone wrong.

The young people listened intently as he explained the daily challenges the police go through to protect the community and keep everyone safe. That meeting turned out to be extremely positive and, to my mind, began building bridges between the local youth and the police. The borough commander left shortly afterwards, and the young people, excited about being listened to, changed their negative mind-sets about the police. Some even considered joining the force in the future.

I was very pleased with the outcome.

Not long afterwards, the borough commander asked me to join the police independent advisory board. This group discusses the day-to-day challenges young people face and recommends ways of dealing with some of these issues. It also makes suggestions on how the police can engage with them, particularly youths from ethnic minorities. For my part, I was able to provide cultural insight that I felt could help avoid conflict between both sides. For example, many African children, especially those from certain West African countries, are raised to evade eye contact with their elders, authority figures and those in positions of leadership. During an interrogation, if a police officer does not understand the significance of this type of behaviour, he or she would assume a young person is hiding something, being deceptive or disrespectful. I also shed light on the passionate outward expressions of black people, such as hand gestures and other body postures that would normally be associated with aggression.

Sharing these and other such information with our local police force helped kick-start a positive relationship between the police and young people in my community. I hope this initiative will be carried out all over the country to reduce unnecessary arrests—particularly among ethnic minorities—to give young people peace of mind, and to create mutual trust and respect on both sides.

I am grateful to and proud of my borough commander and hope for more officers like him who are passionate, charismatic and approachable, particularly with respect to young people. I also hope cultural awareness will be embedded within general police training to foster better understanding of different cultures.

A defibrillator in every school

After the positive results of our meeting with the police, I and the youth of PL9 decided to raise awareness about sudden cardiac death in young people. We sent a proposal asking all the secondary schools represented in the forum to add PL9 to their list of charities, so we could raise money to place defibrillators in schools.

I am now aware that if there was a defibrillator in Philip's school when he collapsed, there is a 75% chance that he would have survived. I also think that if his friends had known about cardiac arrest, they would have called for help much sooner, and the outcome might have been different.

As a result of our campaign, defibrillators have now been placed in fifty-seven schools and public places. In 2013, we raised seven thousand pounds at a charity event, enabling two hundred young people to go for heart screening, out of which, five were diagnosed with heart defects and referred for further investigation. I believe we just might have saved their lives.

Our ultimate goal is to make sure that every school and public place in the country has a defibrillator. We are also pushing for government legislation similar to placing fire extinguishers in every public building. I was very privileged to be invited to the House of Parliament by my local MP, where she passionately debated the importance of defibrillators in schools and public places. She even spoke about the work of PL9 in our community. If your child is aged between 14 and 35, I encourage you to make sure your child goes for heart screening to expose any potential cardiovascular issues. Between 2013 and 2015 I attended the funerals of seventeen young people who died from preventable heart ailments.

Disaster averted!

As I visited and took assemblies in various local schools to raise awareness of sudden cardiac arrest and the need to place defibrillators in local schools, I also began exploring ways to bring the community of young people together to further promote PL9 and Philip's legacy. I asked if the schools could ascertain whether individuals or groups of students would be willing to showcase their talents to their peers and members of their local community. With support from the Headmaster and Philip's Head of Year, we were able to put on a hugely successful show in Bexleyheath Academy in 2013 that has since expanded into an annual event that will soon be taking place in Christchurch, Bexleyheath and Greenwich.

In 2015, PL9 organised a different talent show for local youngsters to exhibit their different skills. As a surprise final act, our local police force was scheduled to put on a musical performance. The idea was to foster community and police engagement, especially among the young ethnic minorities. Towards the end of the event, one of the performers had a suspected cardiac arrest and collapsed on stage. A lot of the audience initially thought this was part of the performance, but panic struck when they realised it wasn't an act. Our new Borough Police Commander promptly sprang into action and performed CPR on the young man. At the same time, while we waited for an ambulance to arrive, his fellow officers went around the local shops trying to get hold of a defibrillator as the venue we used did not have one at the time.

During the incident that night, something humbling also happened-- a number of young people and police officers held hands and prayed for the lad who had collapsed. Fortunately, the young man survived and has now been referred to have further treatment.

Defibrillators placed in schools

From pain to international opportunity

I flew to Africa to visit my elderly mum and relatives in 2014 and we were able to grieve together as a family, since, due to visa restrictions, they were unable to attend his funeral. Our pain worsened when my youngest brother suddenly passed away from a combination of malaria and typhoid in 2015. The shock of losing her grandson and youngest son was too much for my mum and in March 2016, she passed away after a short illness.

I travelled to my home country for the funeral. This sad event turned out to be a huge celebration of her life, with friends and family travelling in from across the country and abroad to pay their respects to a great woman. During my trip, my younger sister, a journalist, arranged for me to speak at an educational conference. After giving a speech on cardiac arrest and demonstrating how to use a defibrillator, I received an open invitation to speak at different schools on the west coast of Africa. This will be a huge opportunity for PL9, and we are currently campaigning for funds to carry out this important work. Sudden death by cardiac arrest affects young people in Africa on a large scale, but due to lack of education and awareness, it is often attributed to witchcraft and demons.   I am grateful that the pain that I have suffered can soon become something of benefit to others in my home country.

No looking back

Back in the U.K. until the government agrees to:

1. making heart screening readily available for young people,

2. the compulsory placement of defibrillators in all public buildings

3. the teaching of first aid as part of the school curriculum

we are not taking any chances at PL9. We have fully dedicated our lives to this cause and other issues that affect young people.

Now you may ask why I had to travel this hard road to be part of this crucially needed change. Well, we often do not understand why things happen the way they do. People of faith might not know *what* tomorrow or the future holds, but when we know and understand *Who* holds our life and futures in His hand, and when we allow His word to help and guide us during our difficult times, we will never go wrong.

I am privileged to have read my Bible from Genesis to Revelation several times before my tragic circumstances took place, and I realise that, when God chooses any of His servants to be part of His divine plan and purpose, He often takes them through significant challenges. When I was going through my darkness, I made sure that my Bible was always close to me, so I could check out the heroes of faith who had gone through similar situations and be encouraged by how they overcame adversity.

One such person was our Lord Jesus Christ. Jesus had to sacrifice his own blood and endure the brutal agony, shame and disgrace of the cross to bring salvation to mankind. It was through his journey to the cross that I was reconciled to God.

The book of Hebrews 12:2 encourages us to have our eyes fixed on Jesus, the guide and end of our faith, who endured the pain of the cross, not caring about the shame, because of the joy which was set before him; and who has now taken his place at the right hand of God's seat of power.

I have often been asked why a good God would allow his only Son to be brutally tortured and killed in order to save other people. How I wish I had the answer, because I have asked the same things myself. None of us will ever understand why, this side of heaven, but I am certain of one thing in my heart—one day we will all have the opportunity to ask Him these questions.

But for now, oh, how grateful I am that Jesus said 'Yes' to the cross. The lyrics of the following song demonstrate what the cross means to me personally:

How deep the Father's love for us,
How vast beyond all measure
That He should give His only son
To make a wretch His treasure

How great the pain of searing loss,
The Father turns His face away
As wounds which mar the chosen One,
Bring many sons to glory

Behold the Man upon a cross,
My sin upon His shoulders
Ashamed I hear my mocking voice,
Call out among the scoffers

It was my sin that left Him there
Until it was accomplished
His dying breath has brought me life
I know that it is finished

I will not boast in anything
No gifts, no power, no wisdom
But I will boast in Jesus Christ
His death and resurrection

Why should I gain from His reward?
I cannot give an answer
But this I know with all my heart
His wounds have paid my ransom

(*How Deep the Father's Love For Us* - Stuart Townend[2])

2   Stuart Townend Copyright © 1995 Thankyou Music (Adm. by Capi-tolCMGPublishing.com excl. UK & Europe, adm. by Integrity Music, part of the David C Cook family, songs@integritymusic.com)

The pain, suffering and sacrifice that Jesus endured for me inspired me to bear my own pain and do what he asked of every believer in the gospel of Mark 8:34 (KJV):

> *When he had called the people unto him with his disciples also, he said unto them, whosoever will come after me, let him deny himself, and take up his cross and follow me.*

I don't know what anyone else's cross is, but I now know mine. I finally realise that taking up my cross and following Jesus is not about going to church every Sunday morning to dance and shout out *hallelujahs* with my hands lifted high to heaven, only to come out a little while later and begin to judge, criticize and condemn those who do not go to the same church or who may not be Christians like myself. I've also realised that taking up my cross and following after the legacy of Jesus is not about attending every prayer meeting, AGM, or deacon and elders meeting; not to mention the *Gossips Committee* meetings. Serving Jesus is to trust Him with my life and do His will for me.

Just for one minute, please!

On the 27th of August 2014, after returning from Orlando for my Certification programme, I was so overwhelmed with negative emotions that I became completely depressed. I missed my son so much on my return, as I wanted him to be at home, waiting to ask me a thousand and one questions about my trip. I kept expecting him to sneak into my bedroom, during the night while I was asleep, to go through my suitcases to discover whether I had brought him back a pair of Adidas trainers from the States. It got so bad that I had to seek medical help.

My doctor prescribed anti-depressant tablets and recommended counselling. I took his advice and attended two counselling sessions. I also took the anti-depressant tablets for three days, but neither helped my situation. Instead, I became even more depressed and developed very strong suicidal feelings. I immediately decided to do something different, as I was not going to allow these potentially destructive emotions to get the better of me by making me do something stupid and cause further pain to my family and friends.

For the next seven days, I withdrew myself from public engagements and shut down all communication with the outside world.

- No phone calls,
- No Facebook,
- No Twitter,
- No Instagram,
- No LinkedIn

That left me, myself and I on the hard wooden floor of my bedroom, with no food but plenty of water for seven days. My request of God for the seven days was to see my son for one minute, to ease my pain. On the seventh day, around lunchtime, as I was praying and crying, begging to see my son, I went into a trance, or, some might say, an out of body experience.

I was all alone, but not afraid, in the middle of a very long and narrow street. Magnificent lights surrounded me everywhere I looked. I have never seen anything like it in my entire life. As I stood there, in complete awe of what I was seeing, a white fog appeared about half a mile in front of me. I averted my eyes from the streetlights and fixed my sights on the gathering mist. Suddenly, somebody stepped out of the fog and started walking towards me.

Guess who that person was? It was my son. *Yes, my baby, Philip!*

I recognised him immediately, because he came out brushing his hair with his hairbrush in his right hand. He was wearing his white Ralph Lauren polo shirt, blue stonewashed jeans, his white and black Adidas trainers, and he was carrying his white and black man-bag. As he approached, he winked at me with a big smile on his face, the kind of smile and wink that he usually gave me whenever I bumped into him hanging around the girls at Bexleyheath Broadway.

I was overjoyed at seeing him and started running towards him, but I noticed that the closer I got to him, the further away he moved, until he suddenly disappeared into the fog. I stood there, confused and upset.

Then I screamed. 'Philip, you can't go! I haven't hugged you yet!'

A voice behind me replied. 'Juliet, you can't touch him.'

'Why not?' I asked, frustrated.

'Because you are in a different place.' The voice replied.

As soon as I heard the words, *you are in a different place*, I woke up, shaking and sweating profusely. At the same time, I realised my prayer request to see my son for one minute had been granted and although I could not touch him, I was satisfied. I will be eternally grateful at how happy he looked.

I also want to encourage anyone who takes the time to read this by letting you know that there is life after death, and it is a beautiful one. My one-minute experience has compelled me to purposefully live my life every day, carefully making positive contributions to this earth so that when I take my exit, I will have the chance to go through that street again. I am also praying that if it is possible, you all have a one minute experience too, because I can testify that seeing truly is believing.

His mighty invisible hand

One beautiful afternoon, I lay in bed gazing at the ceiling, missing my son so much and wishing he would just walk into my bedroom. If only he would come in and tell me it was all a game. I became very emotional, and wept uncontrollably. When I stopped crying, I heard a voice telling me I was a failure and did not deserve to live. Somehow I started to believe what it was telling me.

The voice gave me three options to choose the way I wanted to die.

1. Go to the closest train station and jump into the path of a moving train.

2. Go and jump into River Thames.

3. Die in the comfort of my own home by taking the entire pack of the antidepressants that the doctor had prescribed to me that week.

I agreed with the voice and chose the option of overdosing on antidepressants. Just as I stretched my hand from my bed towards the tablets on my dressing table, I felt a strong hand push me off the bed. I became afraid and ran naked into the hallway. My shock was so great that I almost wet myself. Because I ran out of my bedroom in fear, I forgot to take my phone and could not call anyone. I simply stood there, not knowing what to do. Moments later, it occurred to me to go and visit a friend who works not too far from my house.

When I arrived, the look on her face gave the impression that she was expecting me. She handed me a pile of books containing her after-school pupils' homework. As I read through, some made me cry and some made me laugh. But this particular one, written by an 8-year-old child, touched me deeply. The topic was *How We Can Help God*.

This is how he put it in his own words:

> *I will [sic] like to help God, by listening to God's heart and hear [sic] where God is hurting so I can help him.*

Tears roll down my face even now as I write. On reading this child's account of how to help God, I felt God had just spoken to me. I made my way back home without fear, knelt down beside my bed and began talking to God.

'I have come to do what that little boy said.' I told Him. 'I want to help You, Lord, but I need to listen to Your heart first and see where You are hurting.'

As soon as I said that, an overwhelming pain took over my heart and my body and I began crying like I had never done before. I eventually fell asleep on the floor, and when I woke up the carpet underneath me was completely wet, but all I felt was peace.

I heard a voice whisper. 'Are you still willing to help?'

'Yes, Lord. But what can I do to help?'

'Many of my children are angry with me because they do not know me. But you know me, and they know you, so will you allow me to reach out to them through you? Would you let me meet their needs, love them, embrace and hug them through you?'

'Yes, Lord, with all my heart.'

Immediately, the pain stopped and I became extremely hungry, so I went to the kitchen to prepare something to eat. This incident happened on a Tuesday. On Wednesday, around noon, I had the urge to go to the Broadway, where many students from the area catch their buses home after school. When I arrived at 12.30pm, some boys from Philip's school came over to say hello and asked me what I was doing at the Broadway.

'To be honest, I don't really know.' I told them. 'However, while waiting to find out, I'm going to pop into the bank.'

'Will you come back here when you're done?' One of them asked.

'Definitely.' I said, and went into the bank.

To my amazement when I strolled back from the bank, what seemed like over one hundred boys were queueing on the street, waiting for me. As I made my way towards them, one by one they came up and hugged me. Each hug was different. Some hugged me and left immediately. Some hugged and held me for a few seconds before they let go. Some had tears in their eyes as they hugged me. It was almost an hour before they all left. I stood there and made sure every single one of them had the opportunity to hug me.

People came out from the shops to watch what was going on. After the boys had left, some of those standing around must have thought I was some kind of celebrity. Some summoned the courage to ask who I was.

Why were all these boys hugging me?

I did not know what to say to them, so I just walked away. I got back home and knelt down. 'Thank You, Lord.' I said.

A voice responded. 'Thank you, too.'

Leading by example

I then understood why the psalmist said,

> '*It was good for me to be afflicted so that I might learn your decrees. The law from your mouth is more precious*

to me than thousands of pieces of silver and gold. Your hands made me and formed me. Give me understanding to learn your commands. May those who fear you rejoice when they see me, for I have put my hope in your word.' (Psalm 119:71-74 NIV)

Prior to my own afflictions, I had visited several bereaved families who had lost children or friends. I always offered my condolences but was never able to experience their pain. After my own loss, I now understand what families feel when they lose a loved one, and can identify with them on a deeper level.

Most of my career, I have worked with young people, many of whom shared about their negative encounters with the police with me. At the time, I found it hard to believe some of their stories, but since the incident at my house, I am able to help them positively channel their emotions. I fully understand how they feel and can connect with them.

I learned first-hand through my own experiences and firmly believe that if we want to see change in any area of society, we cannot sit on the fence being angry and bitter and throwing critical stones, expecting improvement to happen just because we make all the right noises. No! We have to volunteer to do what is required by getting involved in the key areas we want to see transformed. By first of all becoming that change, then using the wisdom, knowledge and understanding gained through our experiences, we can begin to introduce the transformation we want to see in our homes, community or country. The process is the same.

Hebrews 4:15 (NIV) says,

> *For we do not have a high priest who is unable to empathise with our weaknesses, but we have one who has been tempted in every way, just as we are—yet he did not sin.*

This is the reason I allow the life and characteristics of Jesus Christ to be my model when dealing with issues. I studied His character during his time on earth and have noticed that he didn't just tell people to change. He modelled change in his lifestyle. He wasn't like some today, who sit in their moral, self-righteous high seats, complaining and telling everyone else what to do, yet never lifting a finger. In spite of Jesus' suffering, pain, and rejection, he stayed fully focused. Never for one day did he complain or blame anyone apart from his critics, the religious leaders. He was a man on a mission to accomplish the will and purpose of God. He remained completely sold out and was irrevocably committed to his purpose, trusting every day in the One who sent him.

His complete dedication and passionate desire to change the lives of the people and community inspired and compelled many people of his day to follow him. Multitudes were transformed through his positive message of change. I am the benefactor of the transforming message Jesus brought over 2000 years ago.

I am forever grateful to the heroes of faith who believed, allowed themselves to be changed and be inspired to take this same life-changing message across the world. As someone born in one of the British West African colonies, I especially want to thank the forefathers of Great Britain, who travelled across many rivers, slept in huts, suffered untold hardship, including mosquito and snake bites to bring this most needed gospel to my motherland.

Without the inner strength I gained from the Bible, I would not have survived all I have gone through in my life and would probably have remained a bitter and angry person forever.

Apostle Paul, one of my role models, encourages us in Romans 12:21 not to be overcome by evil, but to overcome evil with good. I translate it into that famous adage by Dale Carnegie which says *when life hands you a lemon, try to make lemonade.* One of my goals for this book is to help readers understand the power of forgiveness and staying completely free of anger and bitterness. When our mind is transformed, we are able to see our way through even the darkest situations in life.

God has placed creative abilities in every one of his children. We are made in his image and likeness, and his DNA is in every one of us. Just as he created light out of darkness, we can also create light out of our own darkness. But in order to do so, we have to remain constantly connected to Him, because He is the source of our power.

Something that happened to me illustrates this point vividly. One day I bought a new vacuum cleaner at a very reasonable price and decided to test how good it was as soon as I got home. I plugged it in and started vacuuming my carpets. For a few minutes, it was doing a great job, then it suddenly stopped working. I checked that the dust bag was not full; the filter was not blocked, and tried everything I could, to no avail. I became convinced I had wasted my money and started blaming the manufacturer. I went to switch it off at the socket, intending to return it and give the seller a piece of my mind. To my surprise and slight embarrassment, the plug was lying on the carpet next to the wall socket—it had merely been dislodged. I had tugged on the power cable during the test run.

Right there, the Holy Spirit ministered to me, 'Juliet, this is what happens when you are disconnected from me. You become power- less and respond wrongly to everything. As long as you stay connected to me, you will al- ways see positive results out of even the most negative situations.'

I now make sure I am fully connected before I leave for work every morning. I am careful not to react to situations or even respond to anything that would question my charac- ter. Take a look at what Apostle Paul said in Ephesians 6:10-18 (NKJV):

> *'Finally, my brethren, be strong in the Lord and in the power of His might. Put on the whole armour of God, that you may be able to stand against the wiles of the devil. For we do not wrestle against flesh and blood, but against principalities, against powers, against the rulers of the darkness of this age, against spiritual hosts of wickedness in the heavenly places. Therefore take up*

the whole armour of God, that you may be able to withstand in the evil day, and having done all, to stand.

Stand therefore, having girded your waist with truth, having put on the breastplate of righteousness, and having shod your feet with the preparation of the gospel of peace; above all, taking the shield of faith with which you will be able to quench all the fiery darts of the wicked one. And take the helmet of salvation, and the sword of the Spirit, which is the word of God; praying always with all prayer and supplication in the Spirit, being watchful to this end with all perseverance and supplication for all the saints.

He is my source of strength

These scriptures help me every time I face difficult challenges. They have helped me choose my fights; know who I am fighting and use the right weapons each time. I have studied the great heroes of the Bible and observed how they won their battles and challenges. The stories of Naomi in the book of Ruth and Joseph in Genesis 37 are good examples of this.

Ruth – When Life is Not Fair

Theres an old French fairy tale about two daughters—one bad, and the other good. The bad daughter was her mother's favourite, but the good daughter was kind of a 'Cinderella', in that she was unjustly neglected, despised, and mistreated in her own home. One day, while drawing water from the village well, the good daughter met a poor woman who asked her for a drink. The girl responded with kind words and gave the woman a cup of cool water. The poor woman, who was actually a fairy in disguise, was so pleased with the girl's kindness and good manners that she gave her a gift.

She said, 'From now on, each time you speak, a flower or jewel will come out of your mouth.'

Well, when the little girl got home, her mother began to scold her for taking so long to bring the water. The girl started to apologise and when she did, two roses, two pearls, and two diamonds came out of her mouth. Her mother was astonished!

But after hearing her daughter's story and seeing the number of beautiful jewels that came out of her mouth in the telling she called her other daughter, her favourite child (bad, though she was), and sent her out to find the old woman and get the same gift. The bad daughter was reluctant to be seen performing the lowly task of drawing water, so she whined and grumbled sourly all the way to the well. When she arrived, a beautiful queenly woman came by and asked for a drink, this, by the way, was the same fairy in another disguise. Disagreeable and proud, the girl responded with a rudeness that was typical behaviour for her but she received a 'reward' from the fairy as well. Each time she opened her mouth, she emitted snakes and toads.

Now, how's that for poetic justice?

Don't you enjoy stories with that kind of ending? There's something inside us that says, '*yes, that wicked, little, spoiled brat got just what she deserved.'* We like stories like this because in life we want bad people to be punished and good people to be rewarded. We yearn for justice to be done and fairness to reign supreme, but sadly enough, things don't always work out that way, except in the realm of fairy tales. No, in the real world bad **and** good suffer. In fact, it often seems that the wicked prosper while those who do good are ignored or even persecuted. In this life, fairness is a rare thing.

I want us to look at a woman to whom life dealt a very unfair blow. Her name is Ruth and, like Deborah and Hannah, she lived in Israel during the time of the Judges. The four chapters that tell her life story are sandwiched in between the books of Judges and 1 Samuel. And it's easy to find because Ruth is one of only two women who has an entire book of the Bible named after her. The other woman is Esther.

Ruth's narrative has been called the most charming short story in the Old Testament. Even people who are not believers have enjoyed reading this tiny book of the Bible. When Benjamin Franklin was United States Ambassador to France, he occasionally attended The Infidels Club, a group that spent most of its time searching for and reading literary masterpieces. On one occasion, Franklin read the book of Ruth to the club members, but he changed the names in the text so it would not be recognised as a book of the Bible. When he finished, they were unanimous in their praise. They said it was one of the most beautiful short stories that they had ever heard and demanded that he tell them where he had run across such a remarkable literary work. It was his great delight to tell them that it was from the Bible, which they professed to regard with contempt, and in which they felt there was nothing worth reading! Well, let's begin our own study of this story by reading the first 17 verses of the book.

In the days when the judges ruled, there was a famine in the land, and a man from Bethlehem in Judah, together with his wife and two sons, went to live for a while in the country of Moab. The man's name was Elimelech, his wife's name Naomi, and the names of his two sons were Mahon and Kilion. They were Ephrathites from Beth-lehem, Judah. And they went to Moab and lived there. Now Elimelech, Naomi's hus-band, died, and she was left with her two sons.

They married Moabite women, one named Orpah and the other Ruth. After they had lived there about ten years, both Mahlon and Kilion also died, and Naomi was left without her two sons and her husband. When she heard in Moab that the Lord had come to the aid of His people by providing food for them, Naomi and her daughters-in-law prepared to return home from there. With her two daughters-in-law, she left the place where she had been living and set out on the road that would take them back to the land of Judah. Then Naomi said to her two daughters-in-law, 'Go back, each of you, to your mother's home. May the Lord show kindness to you, as you have shown to your dead and to me. May the Lord grant that each of you will find rest in the home of another husband.' Then she kissed them and they wept aloud and said to her, 'We will go back with you to your people.'

But Naomi said, 'Return home, my daughters. Why would you come with me? Am I going to have any more sons, who could become your husbands? Return home, my daughters; I am too old to have another husband. Even if I thought there was still hope for me – even if I had a husband tonight and then gave birth to sons – would you wait until they grew up? Would you remain unmarried for them? No, my daughters. It is more bitter for me than for you, because the Lord's hand has gone out against me!'

At this, they wept again. Then Orpah kissed her mother-in-law good-bye, but Ruth clung to her. 'Look,' said Naomi, 'your sister-in-law is going back to her people and her gods. Go back with her.' Ruth replied, 'Don't urge me to leave you or to turn back from you. Where you go I will go and where you stay, I will stay. Your people will be my people and your God, my God. Where you die I will die, and there I will be buried. May the Lord deal with me, be it ever so severely, if anything but death separates you and me.'

Okay, let's review what has happened so far. Ruth's young husband has died. Her father-in-law and brother-in-law have died as well. Perhaps there was some fever or plague going around, or some accident, I don't know, but all the men in the household are gone. And Ruth's mother-in-law, Naomi, whose name means 'pleasant' and who must have lived up to that name, since she had obviously endeared herself to Ruth and Orpah, well, she has slipped into a deep depression that has caused her to become very cynical. In verse 20, she changes her name to 'Mara,' which means 'bitter.'

Naomi is no longer pleasant. Before all this happened Naomi and her entire family must have had a deep faith in God. In fact, Ruth's father-in-law, Elimelech's name means, 'God is my King.' The family's faith was so genuine, in fact, that it drew Ruth from worshiping the false gods of the Moabite people to following the one True God. But now Elimelech and his sons are dead and his wife seems to have lost her faith. She's angry at God. She blames Him for the unfairness of her situation. So, Ruth—a new believer in God—has gone from being a part of a large, happy, God-worshiping family to being a young widow, alone with an embittered mother-in-law.

And in fairness to Naomi, we should note that she had good cause to be concerned about her situation. These two women were in just about as dire straits as women could be in that male-dominated age, for to be women alone without men was to be faced with ruin. There was no social security in those days, no safety net, no source for any kind of future if a woman didn't have a man in her life. In those days, as Naomi alluded in verse 12, a woman without a man was a woman without hope. So I am sure you will agree that at this point in her life, Ruth had definitely been forcibly enrolled in the school of hard knocks! She had run smack dab into the unfairness of life.

And I think that we should pause here and note that some women today are in a similar situation. Now, they don't live in that kind of male-dominated culture but, like Ruth and Naomi, they are suddenly single. The Bible says that in marriage husband and wife become one and this is not just referring to a physical oneness. There is a spiritual union that takes place, especially in long marriages. If you've had a spouse die then you know that there's a sense in which you feel incomplete, as if half of you were suddenly gone. I've read that it normally takes about two years to become emotionally stable after the death of a spouse. Sometimes it takes even longer.

As the months drag by, widows wonder if their lives will ever be happy and fulfilling again. I've had some tell me that, months after their husband's death, they would think of something during the day and say to themselves, 'Oh, I must tell him about that when he comes home.' But then it would hit them:

'He's is not coming home tonight, or ever.' I've heard of other widows who said they would be singing a hymn in church and suddenly see the back of some man's head that reminded them of their husband. And they would feel the pain of his death all over again. Many of you reading this book may be widows whose husbands died in recent years, and so I know you can identify with Naomi and Ruth in the grief they experienced.

We also have some women whose spouses are still living but have left them, and they are going through the pain of separation or divorce. This is also incredibly agonising. Divorce brings a deep lingering pain. I would say that in a way divorce is more difficult than the death of a mate. There is no closure – no funeral – so the wounds it causes are very slow in healing. If you are reading this today and are dealing with either of these particular types of unfairness, then listen, because I truly believe that Ruth would want you to know some things she discovered that will help you.

1. First of all, I think she would urge you to **cling to the hope that your hurt will ease**.

You may feel like you have an ache in your heart that will never go away, and it may never totally disappear, but it *will* ease. Your life may feel like a long dark tunnel at the moment, but it's not endless. There is light at the end of the tunnel. It may seem like it is far away but it is there. A time will come when you will be able to feel joy once more. Just be patient. The sun will shine again in your life. Remember, it takes far more time for emotional wounds to heal than it does physical ones, but they **do** heal!

Scripture records that there came a time when Ruth and Naomi came to the end of their 'tunnel of darkness.' Ruth met Boaz, a godly man, and they married and he took care of both Ruth and Naomi. Things got better! There was laughter once again in the lives of both of these women. So if you are hurting and alone like they were, then cling to the hope that your pain will ease, theirs did, and yours will as well. And then, another thing that I think Ruth would advise is that you…

2. ….**get involved with life**.

She certainly did. Ruth didn't drop out of life when her husband died. She moved to a strange land and started life all over. And you know, it's not so important what she did, as is the fact that she did something. Ruth stayed busy. She refused to quit on life.

When they arrived in Bethlehem, she heard about the law of gleaning which forbade Israelite landowners to reap their property to the very edge. God's law required them to leave a border of grain standing, so that poor people could gather enough food to survive. Well, Ruth took full advantage of this law, got up, and went to work to find food for herself and Naomi. She didn't quit and go into seclusion. No, she got involved with life. Keeping busy like this – starting over, learning new things, goes a long way toward helping healing begin. And then, I think there is one other thing those who are suddenly single can learn from Ruth…

3. ...and that is **the importance of maintaining their integrity regardless of the situation.**

Ruth certainly did this. In fact, Boaz told Ruth that the thing that attracted him to her was her integrity. Listen to the words of Boaz in verse 11 of chapter 2:

> *'I've been told all about what you have done for your mother-in-law since the death of your husband – how you left your father and mother and your homeland and came to live with a people you did not know before. May the Lord repay you for what you have done.' (NIV)*

You know, many times when people face loneliness they become vulnerable and fall into a physical relationship that is wrong. Some singles get so lonely that they run to the first person they find and compromise their moral standards in their search for something to ease the pain. Many turn to other sinful behaviours and involve themselves in actions that are contrary to God's will. So if you are suddenly single, I urge you to do as Ruth did and guard against this temptation. Do all you can to live a godly life.

In his book, *Hope Again*, Charles Swindoll points out that there are two kinds of bad in this world. There are consequences of living in a sinful world – an unfair world. But there are also consequences of disobeying God, repercussions of ignoring His guidelines. And as a rule, life is fairer for those who try to live God's way. This is what 1 Peter 3:13 (NASB) is referring to when it says, '*Who is there to harm you if you prove zealous for what is good*?' You see, as a general rule, if you live a life of purity and integrity, in the long run, you usually won't suffer as much as those who habitually traffic in evil.

For example, if you pay your debts, chances are good that you won't get into financial trouble. If you pay your taxes on time, you probably won't have the HMRC down on your back. If you take care of your body and get enough sleep and exercise, watch your diet and your stress level, chances are good that you will live a healthier life than those who don't. If you help others, you will probably have someone to help you when you are in need. To paraphrase Peter's verse, 'those who do what is right are usually not in harm's way, *usually*.' Now please hear me in this: we live in a fallen world where the just still suffer unjustly. 'Rain does fall on the good and the bad,' but unjust suffering is always better than deserved judgement. So, in your grief, don't abandon your moral principles, no matter how tempting it may be to do so.

You know, we need to be sensitive to the needs and hurts of women who, like Ruth and Naomi, have lost a spouse unfairly, suddenly. And the story of Ruth is a great place for these hurting people to look for help. But, the wonderful thing about this little book of the Bible is that it also contains principles that will help the rest of us as we deal with other kinds of injustice.

1. For example, one thing all of us can learn from this story is that **it is not always bad to go through bad times**.

Ruth's bad experiences deepened her trust in God. They led her to a new husband and together they had a son who was the grandfather of King David. I believe even Naomi would agree that good came from their bad experiences. You see, often the most valuable lessons of life can only be learned amidst the unfair, the tough times. Listen to what Malcolm Muggeridge had to say in this regard:

> 'Contrary to what might be expected, I look back on experiences that, at the same time, seemed especially desolating and painful, with particular satisfaction. Indeed, I can say with complete truthfulness that everything I have learned in my 75 years in this world, everything that has truly enhanced and enlightened my existence, has been through affliction and not through happiness. In other words, if it ever were to be possible to eliminate affliction from our earthly existence by means of some drug or other medical mumbo jumbo, the result would not be to make life delectable, but to make it too banal and trivial to

be endurable. This, of course, is what the Cross signifies. And it is the Cross, more than anything else, that has called me inexorably to Christ.'

As Muggeridge points out amazing good can come from bad times. If we let God, He will help us experience eternal blessings – even as we go through temporary pain. You see, with God, problems can turn into opportunities for us to grow and mature. So, when unfair times come, we need to trust in God's perspective for, if we allow Him, He will use even these bad times to our advantage.

There are several benefits of tough experiences of life. In trials, our eyes are opened so that we see and understand eternal principles; God's Word becomes more real to us; unfair situations give us a platform of witness to others; and they give us an opportunity to trust God. But the greatest benefit of tough times is when God uses them to shape us more into the image of Jesus. God promised us this in Romans 8:28. Remember its words?

'In all things good and bad God works for the good of those who love Him, who have been called according to His purpose.'

And according to verse 29, that purpose is for us to be *conformed to the image of His Son*. If we let Him, God uses bad times as tools to make us more compassionate, more humble, more patient, more selfless, more like Jesus! So, it's not always bad when bad comes our way, for God can work even the unfairness of life to our good.

In one article of the *Readers' Digest,* there is the true story of Hugh Carrier who, when he was 10 years old, was abducted by a man trying to get even with Hugh's father. The man took him to a secluded spot in the Florida everglades, stabbed him repeatedly with an ice pick, shot him in the head, and then left him for dead. Miraculously, Hugh somehow survived. He was blinded in one eye, but he survived. However, the incident left him emotionally scarred. For years, he never went anywhere alone and could only sleep at the foot of his parent's bed. He was very self-conscious about his injured eye and never smiled. He became insecure and resentful. But when he was 13, Hugh got active in a local Baptist church. He found acceptance and love in the youth ministry there and became a Christian.

One Wednesday evening, at the urging of his friends, Hugh shared his testimony, and as he did, he saw his own horrible experience help others. This caused him to grow deeper in his faith. After high school, he entered Carson-Newman University and graduated with a degree in Psychology and then surrendered to a full-time call to youth ministry and entered Southwestern Seminary in the United States of America. He graduated, married and had three children. God has used him over the years in a powerful way to minister to the unique needs of adolescents.

Eventually, Hugh met his assailant –a man named David McAllister. Police found him in a nursing home, decades after the crime, a feeble, bed-ridden old man. Shortly after they met, McAllister apologised to Hugh for all he had done to him as a boy. And, empowered by the love of God, Hugh forgave him. In fact, he continued to go and visit him. The two became friends. McAllister told Hugh how he had grown up without a father, spending much of his childhood in juvenile halls, and that he was drinking heavily by the time he was a teen. He said he had always considered God to be something only suckers believed in, but with Hugh's help, he began to pray, and before he died, he became a Christian. Hugh said,

> 'What that man did was not the end of my life. It was the beginning. As strange as it seems, that old man did more for me than he could ever have known. For, in his darkness, I found a light that guides me still.'

So Ruth's story can teach us that it is not always bad when bad times come. God can redeem even horrible experiences and make them work for our good.

2. Another thing her experience can teach us is that when unfair times come, **we must not give in to self-pity**.

Ruth and Naomi had two options of how to respond to their unfair situation. One was to wallow in self-pity and bitterness and the other was to face life with optimism and hope. And Naomi chose the former. Listen to her words, *I am too old to have another husband... and even if I did and had sons they'd be too young for you to marry... you're better off leaving me, the hand of the Lord is against me...*

When they arrived in Bethlehem, her friends came out to meet them and noticed her bitterness. They said, '*Can this be Naomi?*' and Naomi says, '*Don't call me Naomi...call me Mara, because the Lord Almighty has made my life bitter.*'

Ray Stedman used to tell the story of an old woman and a preacher. She would come up and list all her problems in life at the end of every service and he would try to give her some positive reason to look at life differently. Her response to the preacher was, 'You know, young man, when God sends tribulations, He expects you to tribulate.'

But Naomi went beyond that. She wasn't just tribulating amidst her tribulations. She had decided that God didn't love her. He loved some people but not her. She believed God had left her and that she was going home to Bethlehem alone and empty-handed. But was she? Was she alone on the way back to Bethlehem? No, there was a young woman named RUTH with her. And as far as God was concerned, Naomi came back with the whole future of the human race holding onto her arm. For, as I said earlier, this young woman would be the mother of Obed, the father of Jesse, the father of David, the King of Israel; ancestor of the Messiah, the Lamb of God who would take away the sins of the world. That's who Naomi came back with. So her hands were far from empty. They were fuller than they had ever been. Yet in her bitterness and self-pity, she couldn't see it.

Now Ruth, the younger, the new believer in God, well, she didn't follow in her mother-in-law's pitiful footsteps. No, instead of the road to self-pity, she chose the road of optimism and hope. She pointed out what they had, not what they didn't have. Ruth knew they still had each other and their relationship with God, and that certainly was something. So she decided to go for life, to glean its simple pleasures, to harvest joy even in a strange land. And this positive attitude was another thing that attracted Boaz to Ruth – he was drawn to her go-get-it work ethic. This is why he instructed his workers to be sure and leave a little extra grain for Ruth to glean.

After they were married, I imagine Ruth discovered his provision. When we choose not to be blinded by self-pity, we can see that God does the same for us. In the midst of our struggle to survive, emotionally, financially, through sickness or bad relationships, whatever it is, if we look, we can see that God does provide for us, just as Boaz did for Ruth.

God misses nothing. He's looking out for us. He's listening to our prayers. 1 Peter 3:12 says, '*The eyes of the Lord are upon the righteous, and His ears attend to their prayer, but the face of the Lord is against those who do evil.*'

Ruth and Naomi's contrasting responses remind me of an old poem my dad used to quote: 'Two men looked through prison bars – one saw mud, the other saw stars.' When you face unfairness in life, be like Ruth look for stars. Don't slip into self-pity.

3. And then perhaps the most important lesson we can learn from Ruth is that when bad times come **we must stay close to God**...

Many times, when we face unfairness in life, we respond much like Naomi, blame God, and give up on Him. We move away from His love, unlike Ruth, who clung to her new-found faith.

In his classic book, *Disappointment with God*, Philip Yancey tells of a man by the name of Douglas who faced a great deal of unfairness in life. His troubles began when his wife discovered a lump in her breast. Surgeons removed that breast, but two years later, the cancer had spread to her lungs. Douglas took over many household and parental duties as his wife battled the debilitating effects of chemotherapy. Sometimes she couldn't keep down any food. She lost her hair and was almost always tired and vulnerable to fear and depression.

One night in the midst of this crisis, Douglas was driving down a city street with his wife and twelve-year-old daughter, when a drunk driver swerved across the centre line and smashed head-on into their car. Douglas' wife was badly shaken but unhurt. His daughter suffered a broken arm and severe facial cuts from windshield glass. But Douglas himself received the worst injury – a massive blow to the head. After the accident, Douglas never knew when a headache might strike. He could not work a full day, and sometimes he would become disoriented and forgetful. Worse, the accident permanently affected his vision. One eye wandered at will, refusing to focus. Due to double vision, he could hardly walk down a flight of stairs without assistance or even read a book.

Yet, he told Yancey that he felt no disappointment in God over his situation. His faith in God was still strong. He said, 'I learned first through my wife's illness and then, especially through the accident, not to confuse God with life.' In other words, Douglas realised that life is unfair, but God is not life. And he refused to let the unfairness of his life push him from God.

You know, we do live in an unfair world. No one is exempt from tragedy and disappointment, and as Yancey reminds us, God Himself was not exempt. His only son, sinless though He was, suffered and died unfairly for the sins of others. Yancey writes, 'At once, the Cross revealed what kind of world we have and what kind of God we have: a world of gross unfairness and a God of sacrificial love.'

Today I invite you to respond to that sacrificial love. If you are reading this book and you are not a Christian then I urge you to trust Jesus today. Ask Him to forgive you of your sin, and to come into your heart and life as Saviour and Lord. I John 1:9 says, 'If we confess our sins, God is faithful and just; He is fair, in that, because of His Son's death on our behalf, He forgives our sins and purifies us from all unrighteousness.

God is a good God, and oh how I wish we all can trust Him with our problems, no matter how big, small or impossible. He is an expert in messy and hopeless situations.

He promised us in the book of Jeremiah 11:29 that his plans for us are not evil, but for good, to give us a hope and a future and, to bring us to an expected end. His expected end for us is far greater and better than any that we might have for ourselves.

Joseph: From Slave to Deputy Pharaoh, a real adventure story

E xperience has taught us that, in large part, that's just not how life works. We know that life is not necessarily a *Choose Your Own Adventure* book. We can't determine how happily ever after our lives will be—or can we? Re-think this with me for a moment. Is it possible that our choices—when it comes to how we decide to respond to life's challenges—is it possible that our 'response choices' can make our lives better or worse? Is there a sense in which life can indeed be a Choose Your Own Adventure? I think the answer is yes, and a validation of this principle is seen in the person who is the 'hero' of the story we are about to read. His name is Joseph.

We are first introduced to Joseph when he was around seventeen years old. He's the son of Jacob, the man God renamed Israel as the forefather of His new nation. Joseph is the grandson of Isaac and the great-grandson of Abraham—and like his great-grandfather, Joseph has quite a story in the book of Genesis. His part of the story begins in Genesis Chapter 37 and runs all the way through to the end of the book. In fact, turn to Genesis 37 and follow along as we look at Joseph's story.

When we read these chapters we learn that Joseph grew up in a very dysfunctional home. His biological mum is dead and he's got three step-mums all living under the same roof. He's got one younger brother and ten older half-brothers and there is a lot of rivalry because Joseph's father, Jacob, or Israel, loves him the most, and everyone in the family knows it. In fact, to show his love for Joseph, Israel gives him an ornate coat—that coat of many colours that I'm sure you've heard about—but it wasn't just a coat. It was a statement. You see, by giving Joseph this coat Israel was saying to his other sons,

> *'Let there be no doubt. This son is my favourite. I love him the most. This son is going to be the main inheritor of my estate. And*

by the way, this is not the coat of a working man, so my son Joseph is not going to do a lot of work out there in the fields He's not going to be doing manual labour. That's up to you less-favoured sons.'

Think about it. It would be like having twelve sons and on Christmas morning you give eleven of them a colouring book from the dollar store and a box of knock-off brand crayons to share but you give the other son an iPad. Lucado writes, 'Joseph got to go to summer camp. His brothers got summer jobs. He got Armani. They got the cheaper stuff.'

The fact is Israel clearly favoured the two sons he had by his beloved Rachel: Benjamin and Joseph—but especially Joseph. As verse 3 says, 'Israel loved Joseph more than any of his other sons,' and I would add, 'loved him more than any of his other sons put together.' I would remind you that Israel learned this poor parenting from his dad. Remember, Isaac had favoured him over his twin brother Esau – and like father, like son, Israel had his favourite.

John Ortberg says that when Joseph's elder brothers walked into the tent, Israel might ask them how the flocks were doing or if they had completed their chores. But when Joseph lifted the tent flap and stood before his ageing dad, Israel's eyes would light up and his face would beam. Joseph was the one Israel bragged about. Joseph got to stay up later, play longer, work less, and get away with more than any of the older sons. Israel knew how Joseph was doing in school. He never missed one of Joseph's soccer games. Israel knew all about Joseph's friends, but he was a little fuzzy about these kinds of details when it came to his other children.

Well, that kind of dysfunctional favouritism always causes problems in a family and it certainly did in Joseph's home. Genesis tells us that his brothers hated Joseph – hated him so much they could not speak a kind word to him.

So, to summarise, Joseph's house was filled with hate, criticism, negativity, and harsh tones. It was not a pleasant place to grow up.

And Joseph didn't help matters. You see, from time to time he had dreams, and he would share them with the family. That wouldn't be so bad if it weren't for the fact that, in his dreams, he was always ruling over his elder siblings. For example, he had a dream of his brothers bowing down to him, and he was foolish enough—spoiled enough—to share that dream with his brothers, which of course only fuelled their hatred of Joseph. Well, one day, Israel sent his well-favoured, dream-interpreting, many-colored-robe-wearing, teenaged son to check up on his brothers when they were tending his sheep. And when they saw him coming, the brothers decided to get rid of this pain in their necks once and for all.

For seventeen years, they had put up with his being pampered, coddled and doted on by their father. And they had had enough. So, they decided to kill him. But Reuben, the oldest brother, talked them out of that, and instead, they did something almost as bad. They sold him as a slave to a caravan of Ishmaelites who passed by on their way to Egypt.

To deceive their father and cover up their horrific act of betrayal they dipped Joseph's special robe in animal blood and showed it to their dad, telling him his favourite son had been mauled by a ferocious animal.

Well, as I said, Joseph's experience shows us that we can't choose our own adventure—we can't choose our families, we can't decide whether or not we'll be thrown into a cistern and sold into slavery, we can't choose our circumstances, but we can choose how we **respond** to those circumstances.

And these choices can make a life-changing difference in the outcome. So there is a sense in which we **can** choose our own adventure, and Joseph's life shows us three ways we can do this.

For example, Joseph helps us to see that we can choose our own adventure...

(1)...in the way we respond to pain or disappointment.

When Joseph arrived in Egypt, he was bought by Potiphar. Scripture says Potiphar was the captain of the Pharaoh's guard—which would make him the equivalent of the Chairman of the Joint Chiefs of Staff. And imagine the painful contrast this was to the way things had been in Joseph's life up until then. For the prior 17 years, he had been waited on hand and foot. Now, here he is in Egypt, not only a stranger in a strange land, but a slave. For the first time, Joseph was experiencing the pain of being away from home, separated from his adoring father, and cut off from all that was familiar. With devastating suddenness, he had gone from being one who was waited upon, to one who waited on others. He'd gone from first place in his father's home to last place in a strange home. Imagine how that must have made him feel. Imagine the culture shock. Imagine having to learn a new language. Think of the loneliness. Think of the anxiety he endured each night as he tried to sleep. He had nothing—no father to protect him, no home, no possessions. Everything he had relied on before was gone.

But, instead of being bitter, Joseph made a faith-filled choice. He chose to respond to this 'adventure' by trusting in God. He didn't indulge in self-pity—and he didn't blame our Heavenly Father. No, he faced all this in the faith that God was allowing this for a purpose. In the midst of an unbelievably bad time, Joseph chose to cling to his faith in God's goodness. Instead of complaining, the Bible tells us that Joseph decided to give himself to serving his new master, and he did this so wholeheartedly that he soon became the most trusted servant in Potiphar's house. Genesis 39:2-3 says,

> *'The Lord was with Joseph and he prospered... the Lord gave him success in everything he did... the Lord blessed the household of the Egyptian, because of Joseph.'*

Do you see what happened? In this time of pain, Joseph's choice lifted him above it all such that he became more aware of God's involvement in his life than he had ever been when he was the spoiled child of his father. When pain came to Joseph's life, he decided to trust God.

And Potiphar saw the evidence of that faith in Joseph's life and labour. He saw that Joseph was a hard-working, diligent young man—a young man who got things done. And this prompted him to increase Joseph's responsibilities and authority. Ultimately, Potiphar put all that he possessed under Joseph's jurisdiction. The Bible says Potiphar '...*did not concern himself with anything except the food which he ate.*' (Gen. 39:6 NASB) So, Joseph went from being a common slave to running the household of the top military man in Egypt. This would be like a cleaner at number ten Downing Street later becoming the Prime Minister of Britain.

Listen. Life almost never turns out the way we expect. Painful times come to all of us. The rain falls on the just and the unjust, and when we get to that inevitable painful 'page' in our lives, we have a choice to make. We can give in to despair or we can trust God and embrace hope. We can become bitter or, with God's help, we can become better. We can give up— or we can get up and go forward. And our decision on this; the choices we make when the adventure of life turns painful can make all the difference to what will happen next.

I mean, even though Joseph's dreams turned into a nightmare, he decided on the correct response. He could have said, *'This isn't what I signed up for. I may have to work for this man, but I don't have to like it. I'll work with a negative spirit. I'll punch the clock. I'll go through the motions but I'm definitely not going to give it my best. Why should I?'*

One of the key phrases in the story of Joseph's life is in Genesis 39:2 where it says, '*The Lord was with Joseph.*' You see, it was when life did not turn out the way he thought it would that Joseph discovered he was not alone. It was in a distant land, far from home, far from his father, far from his family, that he realised that somebody was with him from whom he could not be separated, and that someone was God! What if Joseph had not seen this? What if he made the choice to close his eyes to God's presence? What if he had just given in to despair and quit? There's a good chance he would have missed his destiny. He would have missed the unique role that God had chosen for Joseph to play in His story – His redemptive plan.

Of course, the truth is that, as one of God's people, He has chosen every one of us to play a unique role in the redemption of the world. When we give up, when we give into pain and despair, we miss out on the joy of doing unique things.

Let me stop and ask; have you ever quit doing something significant when the going got tough?

A show of hands on this one, how many of you ever took piano lessons when you were growing up? How many of you ever quit before you could play like Marilyn? Raise your hands. I did. I wish I hadn't but I did. It was just too hard and my schedule was just too busy. Listen friends. Here's the truth we must embrace: quitting is always easier than enduring. Ortberg writes,

> 'It's always easier to stop and have a doughnut than run another lap. It's always easier to stomp out of a room in anger than stay and do the hard work of seek-

ing to resolve a conflict. It's always easier to gossip about someone than it is to go to them and fix things. When life does not turn out the way we planned, the option of quitting begins to look like sweet relief.'

Here are some examples. As husbands and wives, we all discover that marriage is difficult at times. Well, many spouses think, '*I didn't sign up for this. It's too hard. It's too painful. I want out.*' And they get a divorce. Others stay married but they give up on the relationship and settle for mediocrity. They think, '*I'll just give up pursuing oneness. I'll just quit, outwardly or inwardly. That's the easy way.*'

Here's another example. People want to live on a budget and honour God with their giving, by tithing and being financially disciplined, but when it gets hard, they think, '*I'm just tired of the effort. I want to buy the latest iPhone like everyone else. I'm just going to spend. I'm just going to buy what I want when I want. That's the easy way.*'

Well, there's the problem with quitting like this. It may bring us temporary relief, but it tends to produce people who live in a pattern of just giving up. And every time you face some painful situation and choose to quit it shapes your character a little bit. It forges your personality such that it makes quitting a little bit easier the next time. On the other hand, pattern character gets forged when you are like Joseph in that you decide to trust God and endure even though you feel like quitting.

People in whom the faith grows strong are people who say, '*I will seek to grow and persist and be wholly faithful, even in painful circumstances that I don't understand.*' That's the kind of thing that builds great churches, great marriages, great Christians, and great families. It happens when people just buckle down and say, '*even though life has not turned out the way that I planned, even though I'm disappointed in this situation, I want to be like Joseph so I'm going to refuse to quit. I'm going to devote myself wholeheartedly, as the Scripture says, to whatever my hand finds for me to do.*'

When we do that, we discover something. We discover that the Lord is with us where we are, even in a distant land, even in slavery, even in some painful chapter of our life, even when a dream has failed and life seems more like a nightmare. If you decide not to quit and instead to endure and do your best you will learn that you are not alone. God is with you. That realisation makes all the difference because God helps you find meaning even in your difficulty and disappointment. He grows you, matures you, makes you into a better person. And that experience is a great adventure, indeed.

A second lesson Joseph's life teaches us when it comes to choosing our own adventure is seen in the choices we make...

(2)... in the way we decide to respond to the temptation of Passion.

In Genesis 39:6 it says, 'Joseph was handsome in form and appearance.' The NIV translates it, 'Joseph was well-built.' Please understand. There is nothing wrong with being physically well-built or handsome. But with these unique attributes come unique temptations. Now, at this point in his life, Joseph had just about everything: power, authority, respect. He was a house servant who had it made: his own private quarters, access to very confidential information, and the complete trust of his powerful employer. On top of that, he was a good-looking man who, without intending to do so, caught the eye of women. And because of this, things went downhill for Joseph. In verse 7 it says, *'And it came about after these events that his master's wife looked with desire at Joseph and she said, 'Lie with me.''*

She definitely took the direct approach, didn't she? This woman boldly, brazenly, shamelessly came right out and said, 'Come to bed with me Joseph. Let's have a fling.'

Many other men both then and now would have been caught off guard and, at least momentarily, would have felt flattered by such a seductive statement—flattered enough to succumb. Plus—let's be honest. Life had not been fair to Joseph. Things hadn't turned out the way he wanted. In spite of his position, he was still a slave in a strange land. Life was disappointing.

And, many times, disappointments like these lead us to justify our disobedience to God.

We say,

> *'God is not holding up His end of the deal. I mean, look where I am. This isn't how the story was supposed to unfold. Since God has let me down, I'm not obligated to obey His law. I'm justified to have a little fun – sin a little.'*

I think this is especially true of sexual sin, and unfortunately, this is how many singles whose lives are disappointing begin to think. They try things God's way and Mr or Mrs Right doesn't show up, so they are tempted to give up on their Biblical morals when it comes to the pleasures of physical intimacy. I read this week that, when asked what the number one temptation singles face is, 90% said, 'sex.' The other ten percent said, 'lying.' Seriously, many singles think, *'I've tried it*

God's way and it's not working. I'm alone and lonely. I'm tired of going to other people's weddings. So I'm going to try it my way. I'm going to have a little fun. After all, I'm not getting any younger.'

Singles are susceptible to this sinful way of thinking, but married people struggle here, too. Spouses who become disappointed with their marriages use that to justify flirting with a co-worker or an old boyfriend online. The fact is, disappointments have a tendency of justifying our disobedience.

Joseph's story wasn't turning out the way he thought it would so he could have gone in that direction. He could have made the choice to disobey God and have a little fun. But, as Joseph got to the bottom of this page of his life, he didn't take that option. No, he made the right choice. Look at verses 8-9 (NASB):

'He refused and said to his master's wife, 'Behold, with me here, my master does not concern himself with anything in the house, and he has put all that he owns in my charge. There is no one greater in this

house than I, and he has withheld nothing from me except you, because you are his wife. How then could I do this great evil, and sin against God?'

Now, did you notice Joseph's tactic? He simply refused! He said no. How could he do that? What gave him the power to make this choice, to resist that kind of temptation? Our answer is in the last sentence of verse 9 where Joseph says to Mrs Potiphar, '*How then could I do this great evil with you—and sin against God*?' Do you see? Joseph's faith relationship with God was the 'lever' that gave him the strength to pry himself away from this woman's seductive grasp.

Over the years in Egypt, his relationship with God had become too important; too valuable to him to do this kind of thing. But Potiphar's wife didn't take no for an answer. Look at verse 10: 'And it came about as she spoke to Joseph day after day that he did not listen to her to lie beside her or be with her.' Clarence Macartney says,

'This was no ordinary temptation. Joseph was not a stone, a mummy, but rather a red-blooded young man in his late 20's. It was not one temptation on one day, but a repeated temptation. An old story tells how when Joseph began to talk about God to the temptress, she flung her skirt over the bust of the stone idol that stood in the chamber and said, 'Now God will not see.' But Joseph answered, 'My God always sees.''

And friends, HE DOES and Joseph knew this. He said no to this woman because he had come to see that God was indeed always with him. By now—thanks to a painful set of circumstances—God had become more real to Joseph than anything or anyone else on earth. And Joseph was able to resist Potiphar's wife's repeated advances because of this reality.

If you are confronted with temptation like this, and you manage to resist, and then think that this temptation will somehow vanish, think again. In fact, thinking we are invulnerable to temptation makes us an even greater target for the tempter. That kind of pride is like painting a target on our chest. We should keep in mind that Satan wants the respected person. He wants to trap the person who is quoted by others—the successful individual—the trusted partner—the Godly soul.

Satan wants people like this to yield to temptation for when they do, everyone notices, and this is why it is no surprise that Potiphar's wife went after Joseph with such relentless persistence. I mean, Joseph was a catch. If she got him, she would have conquered something! But, praise God, Joseph chose to say no. Before the words were even written in God's book, Joseph obeyed 1 Timothy 6:11 where it says, '*Flee from immorality.*'

We would be wise to do the same when we turn a page in life and face similar temptations. By the way, anyone who didn't choose to flee would tell you they regret their foolish decision. They regret giving in to passion. They regret destroying their family, alienating their children, negating their witness.

So, to summarise, Joseph shows we can choose our own adventure in the way we respond to pain and to the temptation of passion; and then his example also shows us the difference we make…

(3) …in the way we decide to respond to Power.

You remember what happened. When he refused the invitation of Potiphar's wife and fled, she lied and accused him of raping her. Because of these false charges, Joseph was thrown into prison. Now, one of Potiphar's jobs as Captain of the Pharaoh's guard was to Chief Executioner, and the favourite way to execute people back then would have been to bury them alive. This was one of the options for those accused of rape. Since Potiphar didn't sentence Joseph to this horrible death we can be pretty sure that he trusted Joseph more than he trusted his wife. With this lighter sentence, Potiphar saved face and Joseph spent the next ten years in prison—but while he was there his God-given gift of understanding dreams became very useful.

Two of his fellow prisoners had dreams, and with God's guidance, Joseph interpreted them. One of those prisoners was the cup-bearer to the Pharaoh. Soon the cup-bearer was freed and, two years after that, Pharaoh had a dream. He needed someone to interpret it, and the cup-bearer recommended Joseph. Joseph interpreted the Pharaoh's dream to mean that seven years of abundant harvests were coming throughout the land of Egypt, but seven years of famine would follow. Joseph followed God's guidance and suggested storing the surplus of food during the abundant years so they would have food for the years of famine.

In his interpretation of Pharaoh's dream, Joseph repeatedly referred to God as the source of the interpretation. In other words, Joseph didn't call attention to himself. No, he gave all the glory to God. And this apparently impressed Pharaoh. In Genesis 41:39-40 (NASB) he said,

> *'Since God has informed you of all this, there is no one so discerning and wise as you are.*

You shall be over my house, and according to your command all my people shall do homage; only in the throne will I be greater than you.'

So, do you see what happened? Pharaoh made Joseph in charge of the whole land of Egypt. In 13 years Joseph went from a slave in a foreign land to being a ruler in that land; and not just a ruler—Joseph was second only to Pharaoh himself. Genesis 41 says that Pharaoh took off his signet ring and put it on Joseph's finger. Think of this ring as the platinum charge card of the day. It was the way the king stamped the invoices, the laws, or anything else he wanted to verify or validate with his seal. With this ring, Joseph wore the authority of the Pharaoh's imprint.

Along with this, Pharaoh gave him fine garments made of linen and placed a gold necklace around his neck. He was even given a royal chariot! Now think about it. Only a few hours before, Joseph was a scruffy, ragged, and forgotten prisoner in the dungeon. I guess you could call him, 'Cinder-fella' because he instantly went from prisoner to prince.

Well, how could this happen? It's because our Sovereign God was writing the story. God prefers to use unlikely people to work out His plans, like using an elderly infertile couple to populate an entire nation. The time came for God to rescue that nation—His chosen people—because a famine was coming. He needed one of His people in a position of authority and power. So He chose a former slave, an ex-convict—named Joseph, another unlikely character in God's story. God used Joseph to execute a plan that saved millions of people all over the world from starvation. You see, the famine didn't just affect Egypt. It spread to other nations including Canaan where Joseph's father and family—the beginnings of God's nation—needed food.

Jacob sent Joseph's older brothers down to Egypt to buy grain. When they arrived, they met Joseph but didn't recognise him. They bowed down to him—remember the dream? Joseph put them through a few tests to see if they had changed, to see if they were sorry for what they did. But after a while, he could no longer keep up the act and he broke down in tears and introduced himself to his brothers. Think of it. He is in a position of unquestioned power over these guys. He could have chosen to use his power to have them tortured and executed. When he turned the page of his life and found his brothers at his mercy—the men who had sold him into slavery—he could have decided to make them pay. But he took the other option. He acted compassionately toward them. He decided not to use his power to hurt them.

Instead, he brought them, his dad, and the whole dysfunctional clan to Goshen and provided for their every need. And then years later when his dad died and his brothers thought that surely, now Joseph would use his power to take his vengeance he told them, *'You guys have no worries. I love you! You're my brothers. Yes—you did me wrong, and you meant it for evil, but God meant it for good.'*

Joseph chose to use his power to be compassionate, to forgive. And the thing that gave him the wherewithal to do this was the fact that he could look back and see that the one true God who had been with him, had worked in all that bad—the slavery, the prison term—God had worked in all that bad for his good and for the good of God's chosen nation. He saw that God had redeemed his life at every turn of the page.

Listen, friends, we must never give up on God redeeming our story no matter what disappointments and failures we face in life. God is the great redeemer. He can redeem anything. It's never too broken, never too late. God can fix anything. He can make something beautiful out of any life, no matter how many disappointments it contains. As Paul puts it in Romans 8:28, *'In **all things**, God works for the good of those who love Him and are called according to His purpose.'* And when Paul says all things, he means all things—good things, bad things, painful things, disappointing things, health problems, relational problems, financial struggles, marital struggles, **ALL THINGS**.

Heroes that inspire us

Here are some heroes of our generation who stayed connected to Him through thick and thin. He has transformed nations through them such that their lives and legacies will for ever remain in the hearts of many.

Mother Teresa Quote

'By blood I am Albanian, by citizenship Indian, by faith I am a Catholic nun, as to my calling, I belong to the world. As to my heart, I belong entirely to the heart of Jesus'.

Martin Luther King JR Quote

'Well, I don't know what will happen now. We've got some difficult days ahead. But it doesn't matter to me now. Because I've been to the mountaintop. And I don't mind. Like any man, I would like to live a long life. Longevity has its place. But I'm not concerned about that now. I just want to do God's will. And He's allowed me to go up to the mountain. And I've looked over. And I've seen the Promised Land. I may not get there with you. But I want you to know tonight, that we, as a people will get to the Promised Land. And I'm happy, tonight. I'm not worried about anything. I'm not fearing any man. Mine eyes have seen the glory of the coming of the Lord'.

Nelson Mandela Quote

'As I walked out the door toward the gate that would lead to my freedom, I knew if I didn't leave my bitterness and hatred behind, I'd still be in prison.

Juliet's Reflections

I asked myself last night.

How have I managed without my Philip?

How have I managed without his beautiful smile that brightened up my day?

How have I managed without our daily 5pm hugs whenever we had the chance?

How have I managed without his cheeky way of asking for money for new trainers and for his weekly hair shape up?

How have I managed without my lovely cup of tea and the beautiful toast he made me at the weekend?

How have I managed without the boxes of chocolates you bought me at Christmas, New Year and for Mother's Day, even though you would eat them yourself because you wanted to 'share the love'?

How have I managed without the prayers and encouragement you always gave me after telling me off for saying or doing something wrong?

How have I managed without my Philip?

I think I can say I have managed, because although you left, you did not leave me comfortless. You left me with the best of your friends, who have not left my side. They have stood with me and together we are still standing! With your help, the love and unity we have built will continue to bind us together.

I want to thank God for his grace and mercy that has helped me through. Love you so much and missing you like crazy, but trusting every day you are in His everlasting arms.

Memories

> *For the Lord himself shall descend from heaven with a shout, with the voice of the archangel, and with the trump of God: and the dead in Christ shall rise first: then we which are alive and remain shall be caught up together with them in the clouds, to meet the Lord in the air: and so shall we ever be with the Lord.* (1 Thessalonians 4:16-17 KJV)

This Scripture and my memories give me joy and hope. One day, I will be reunited with my handsome young man in the sweet by and by where there will be no more sickness, pain or injustice.

Let me go back to the beginning.

A year before I became pregnant with Philip, I asked God to give me a male child that I would raise to the best of my ability. I also pledged to give him back to God. I made this vow in my naivety as a Christian, without really understanding the cost of such a promise. Had I realised I would have to pay up so soon, I would have done things differently. I would have made sure I enjoyed every moment with my son as I took the time to train him to be a role model and grow up into the true man of God he turned out to be.

I remember how thrilled I was when the doctor finally told me I was pregnant. I was probably the happiest woman on earth.

A few months into my pregnancy, however, the doctor told me my baby was a girl. I asked God whether he had forgotten that my request was for a boy. When God did not respond, I made no fuss about it. All I wanted was a healthy child.

I was so full of joy that I immediately started shopping for baby clothes. Four months into my pregnancy I would wake up every morning, get dressed and make my way to different shopping centres in the city where I lived in Germany. I would shop for baby clothes from the early hours of the morning until the store attendants informed me that they were about to close for the day. By the sixth month of my pregnancy, my baby shopping was completed. Everything was purple and pink, including the colour of the baby's room and cot.

In the eighth month, I experienced a sharp pain in my stomach and decided to get myself checked out. The doctor carried out another ultrasound, but this time he looked surprised and signalled for two other doctors and a nurse to join him.

'What's happening with my baby?' I didn't want to panic but being surrounded by four medical practitioners, when there would normally be one doctor and a nurse was beginning to concern me.

'Everything is alright with your baby,' the doctor hastily assured me. In fact, he and his colleagues seemed to be amused by something. 'There is a little surprise for you, though.'

'What surprise?' I had no idea what to expect at this stage.

'You're having a baby boy!' He said, still smiling. 'I think he's going to be a cheeky young man.'

'Why do you say that?'

'Well, we've studied the previous ultrasound scans again, and it appears he had his hand over the middle section of his body each time, which is why we concluded he was a girl.'

I looked up and smiled, knowing that my prayers for a boy had been answered. The doctors didn't know about my conversation with God, but God and I knew what had happened, which was all that mattered. On the 18th of November 1996, my baby finally arrived. His original due date was the 22nd of November. As soon as he was handed to me, I lifted him up and worshipped and thanked God for keeping to his side of the bargain. I also asked Him for the grace to keep my own part of the bargain.

A month after Philip's birth, I took him to church and dedicated him to God, and from that time on he never left church or shied away from Christians. When he was little, all I had to do was put some worship music by Ron Kenoly or Don Moen, hand Philip his feeding bottle and he would sit there content-edly while I carried on with my housework. He even loved going to church to the extent that he would cry if I chose not to attend. Philip was a devoted and passionate young Christian.

On the 16th of December 2000, we moved from Germany to the UK. At first, it was very difficult to find a church we could settle in, which he found upsetting. In April 2002, we finally found a wonderful church where we were both welcomed, and that soon became home to us.

Philip loved our new church so much that, every Sunday morning, he woke up early to make sure we were not late for what was only a ten-minute walk from home. As soon as we arrived, he would immediately look for Vicky Kot, to whom he quickly became attached. Vicky would take him to Sunday school and make him sit with her, like the big sister he never had. Philip loved all the attention.

In 2004, a visiting minister from India came to preach at the church. During the sermon, I felt a hand on my shoulder. It was Philip.

'Mum, I want to give my life to Jesus.' He said, looking at me with tears in his eyes.

I was shocked—my son was only eight. 'Do you understand what it means to give your life to Jesus?'

He did not answer, but the tears kept streaming down his face.

'Alright, why don't we talk to Pastor?'

Philip nodded.

I approached my Pastor at the front of the church and passed on Philip's request. He was so pleased he suggested Philip be given the opportunity to give his heart to the Lord there and then. So, at eight years of age, Philip went to the altar and received Christ as his Lord and Saviour. A month later, as he rose out of the water after being baptised, he was the happiest lad I had ever seen.

Little did I know that he was being prepared for his journey. After his baptism, Bible Challenge became our favourite Mother and Son game. We would pick out and memorise whole psalms from the Bible, and Philip would almost always be the first to complete any task we set ourselves. One month, to my amazement, he memorised Psalms 23, 27 and 91. These three Psalms went on to become his favourites. Every weekday, we would hold hands and recite Psalm 23 when I dropped him off at school, Psalm 27 when I picked him up, and Psalm 91 at bedtime.

Just before he turned eleven, Philip announced that a friend's mother had allowed him to have a tattoo for his eleventh birthday, so Philip wanted a piercing *and* a tattoo for his own eleventh birthday.

'Do you know what the eleventh commandment says, Philip?' I asked him. '"Thou shall neither pierce nor tattoo thy body".'

He stared at me briefly, nodded and said no more about it. By the age of eleven, Philip had read his Bible from Genesis to Revelation. One morning, he cornered me.

'Mum, I can only find ten commandments, not eleven.'

'The eleventh one must be in there somewhere, Philip.' I retorted. 'Do your research.'

I thought that would be the end of it, but I underestimated my son. He came home from school that day, sat on the settee and looked at me with a twinkle in his eye.

'Mum, I asked my R.E teacher where the eleventh commandment is in the Bible. Apparently, you must have the African Parents' Bible, because he said there is no such thing as an eleventh commandment!'

The doctors were right. Philip was a cheeky chap indeed.

Letters to Philip

To Philip Lamin

Happy 18th Birthday to the most precious, beautiful, handsome, caring, charming, loving, cheeky young man I had the privilege of living with for 16 great years.

Your short, impressive and inspiring life did not leave with you, but has continued with me, your friends, our family, the staff at your school (Bexleyheath Academy) and the entire community of Bexley Borough.

So, my dearest Philip, even though your life was cut short, your legacy and cute smile remain fresh in the minds of so many, and this is what I am holding onto. Waiting with expectation for that glorious day when my 'roll will be called up yonder', and I shall see you by that beautiful pearly gate, waiting to show me round and tell me what you have been up to since you left us.

I decided to post this picture of you and your favourite Auntie (as you fondly called her), plus your sweet little cousin. Seeing you kissing your cousin made me wish I had the opportunity to kiss my grandchildren from you. But it is okay, the will and purpose of your Maker and mine must come to pass.

So, my dear son, though I am writing you this note with hot tears streaming down my face, I am also making a choice to celebrate what would have been your eighteenth today.

Dearest Philip, with permission from neighbours, I am raising the roof, and will have a blazing praise and worship party to keep those charming eyes of yours happy. I am remembering you showing off your whiter-than-white teeth while brushing your hair at the same time, you're so cheeky!

I am also very sure you will be having one massive firework of a party up there with all the saints today.

So my precious, till we meet again, goodbye, adios, *Auf Wiedersehen*, and yes, son, I am still keeping the vow I made to you on your last day. I can even renew it again with you right now. With every conviction in my heart,

I am giving every hour, every day, every week, every month and every year of the rest of my life to mentoring your friends, and making sure they get to enjoy their lives. I want them to fulfil their God-given potential. I am also fighting to maximise the chances of cardiac arrest survival for the next generation. I am making it my life's work. I refuse to live another day measuring my life by the duration of time I live on this earth. But I am going to live every day finding ways of making a contribution; so that this world becomes a better place for your friends and the next generation.

I am working, watching, praying and looking to all of you upstairs for daily strength, courage and wisdom.

All my Love, MUM.

To my dear son , and dearest friend. I just wanted to let you know I'm thinking of you on the eve of your 17th Birthday, and would like to have been with you and your new team on your glorious birthday celebration. I want you to know we will be celebrating down here with you. Even though I miss you so much and would have loved to have you here with me so we can continue to celebrate and do all the things we like doing on our individual birthdays, I have to surrender to our Maker's will and purpose as I see all you are still achieving even in your absence. This has helped to ease the pain of you not being here with me in person.

I want to let you know that the penny has finally dropped. You always told me you wanted loads and loads of brothers and sisters, as long as they didn't enter your room or touch any of your stuff without your permission. Well, as you already know, you now have more of them than you would ever have thought possible.

I hope you and the Big Guy up there are planning the mansion to keep all of them! I also want to assure you that so far, none of them has entered your room or touched your stuff without permission. They are just as well-behaved as you, so I want to thank you for setting that standard. Thank you for also teaching me what true friendship should look like.

I will always be so proud and honoured to be called Philip Lamin's mum. Please continue to remind us of what your life and death have given us. UNITY. And please help us continue to strive to preserve and maintain it regardless of the misunderstandings and challenges we go through, because together we stand and divided we fall!

All my love to you. I miss you, my son, my friend and my mentor.

You will be forever loved.

Happy Birthday, Philip.

From Mum xx

Dear Lord, as I sit here trying to relax, I reminisce over the last ten months, remembering that You took back from me that which Your very hand gave.

You clearly stated in Your word that every good and perfect gift comes from You, and as a mother to Philip, I can testify that Philip was a good and perfect gift to me, a good and loyal companion to his friends, and a good citizen to the community he grew up in. Even though I have missed him terribly over the ten months since You took him to be with You, and especially during the phase I am about to enter into—like my first Christmas without him—I know it will not be easy, but I am choosing to celebrate for him. This is what he would want, since we both know the importance of Christmas, because, over two thousand years ago, You gave Your only son as a gift to us, so that someone like me could have a relationship with You.

Today, as I think about Your son Jesus and my son Philip, all I can say is that it made me fall in love with You all over again; so instead of sitting here and feeling somewhat sorry for myself, I am going to celebrate this Christmas in style, by renewing my love vow to You all over again.

I want You to know, Lord, that I love You so much and unconditionally, with all my heart, and nothing can stop me loving You. No angel or person, life or death, principality or power, or anything in heaven or on earth has any chance of separating me from You. My love for You is for better, for worse, in sorrow and in pain. All I ask, from both You and Philip, is that You continue to grant me all the strength I need, to enable me do my work here on earth. Not just to do it, but to finish well.

In conclusion, Lord, please bless everyone that has stood with me, encouraged and supported me on this journey over the past ten months.

Surprise every one of them this Christmas; give each of them the biggest teddy bear hugs they have ever received. Fill their hearts with joy and laughter this Christmas and above all, may we all experience the reason for the season.

I love You Lord, because You first loved me.

JULIET LAMIN – Outstanding Achievement Award

Even though my name is on the award, I want it publicly known that this honour has only been achieved by the hard work and dedication of the young people who have passionately driven PL9 and my son's legacy forward till date.

The media frequently portrays young people, particularly those from ethnic minorities, so negatively. I want to encourage everyone to engage with young people, so we can demonstrate our belief in them, tap into their passion and vision for the future, and help them become great leaders of tomorrow.

In February 2013, Juliet Lamin lost her only son, suddenly and tragically, through sudden cardiac arrest (SCA). Philip was playing football after school when he collapsed and passed away. Philip was 16 years of age and had no previously diagnosed heart conditions.

The days that followed were like no other we had ever encountered. Juliet visited the Academy daily. Despite her own devastating grief, she came every day with dignity and pride to support not only Philip's friends, but also the staff who were facing a huge loss. Her overwhelming aim was to ensure that **we** were okay. Despite her own obvious grief, she was determined to support anyone she could in any way.

Juliet's last promise to her son was that she would look after his friends, something she has taken to much wider proportions than anyone could envisage at that time.

Shortly after Philip passed away, Juliet set up a youth group, launched in the weeks following his death, for his friends and community. PL9 was born, based in Bexley. Throughout this period, Juliet has put her own grief, anguish and sorrow to one side and been there for all her son's friends who have been finding it difficult to process what really happened on the 5th of February. She opened her home to all the children, and her house became a place for her son's friends to revise for their exams, as her desire to help Philip's friends remained strong.

Juliet may have lost her only child, but she has now become a 'mum' to over four hundred 15 to 19 year-olds.

PL9

PL9 is an open forum for 15 to 19-year-old teenagers in memory of Philip. A place where they can all be together and talk about issues pertaining to teenagers in a friendly, open environment. Juliet and a group of Street Pastors oversee the forum. Issues discussed include personal safety, wellbeing, future goals and many other current issues.

Nobody has ever had such a profound effect on Bexleyheath Academy the way Juliet Lamin has. Since Philip passed away in February, her thoughtful and tireless campaigning to raise awareness of sudden cardiac arrest in our youth has been incredible. Her dignity and determination is humbling to all who meet her. A generation will grow up with Juliet as a guide and mentor, a mother and a fighter. Juliet is the embodiment of the fight against the injustice to parents and friends who have lost a young person at the prime of their life to a terrible, unpredictable tragedy.

The answer to sudden cardiac arrest lies in three forms:

- Cardiac Screening
- the provision of defibrillators in all public places
- Juliet Lamin

Juliet has embraced these resolutions and is so determined that, in the 7 months since Philip passed away, she has worked determinedly to raise the awareness of the wider population about this silent killer, and more significantly, to realise her dream and lasting legacy in Philip's name—a defibrillator in **every** secondary school in the Borough of Bexley.

Juliet has been tirelessly writing to and meeting with anyone she believes can support her campaign to raise awareness. She has been invited on separate occasions to have lunch with the Mayors of Bexley and Greenwich, where she took the opportunity to apprise them of her campaign and how she hopes to realise its fruition.

In addition, in the same very short space of time Juliet has:

- Assisted in the organisation of 'Woolwich Youth Together Community Cohesion' – an event attended by over 3000 young people

- Taken part in the 'Flatline' documentary to raise national awareness of sudden cardiac arrest, where she spoke frankly about the pain and loss of her only son and called for the government to fund screening for all young people aged 14-35

- Started on a journey of fundraising, commencing with a memorial football match, which raised sufficient funds for Bexleyheath Academy to undertake 2 full days of Cardiac Screening in February 2014

- Acquired, through campaigning, two defibrillators for Bexleyheath Academy

- Participated in a 12-mile walk around London for C. R. Y (Cardiac Risk in the Young) to raise funds and awareness

Tragically, exactly four months to the day of Philip's death, Bexleyheath Academy suffered the loss of another young pupil. Reeling from the shock, the very first thing Juliet did was to call the school to check that we were okay. Juliet appeared at the Academy the following day to support those who had supported her, and for the following two weeks supported them in whatever way she could. Guiding, talking, listening and keeping them focused on their exams. Once again Juliet's resilience came to the fore, and her overwhelming urge to put her pain and loss to one side and support others was evident. When asked why, her reply was simple:

'It is very challenging for me, but I have to be strong for them. I have just got to carry them through because they need me to support them. I feel privileged that they trust me and are able to talk to me.'

Juliet Lamin says she will focus the rest of her life on a foundation in Philip's name to raise awareness of the dangers of sudden cardiac arrest, emphasising how it can be prevented, and also, to put in place a defibrillator for every secondary school in Bexley Borough.

She said, 'I want to minimise the deaths of young people full of potential. I wouldn't want any other mother to go through what I have. Not having a chance to say goodbye is just too much.'

Juliet has since raised, through various channels, sufficient funds to purchase another defibrillator and is starting, slowly but surely, through commitment and dedication to realise her dream of placing a defibrillator in every secondary school in the Borough of Bexley. Her actions, in those dark days following Philip's untimely death, are outstanding. They are a phenomenal achievement for someone who has lost so much.

Through Juliet Lamin's selflessness, determination and courage, the youth of the borough stand an increased chance of survival, should the unthinkable ever happen again. Her determination that schools should have correct equipment and training to save a life and prevent another family and community feeling her pain is beginning to emerge into reality.

We at Bexleyheath Academy believe Juliet Lamin has displayed remarkable determination and courage, giving unselfishly of her time, voluntarily and in good grace, to support the youth within the Borough of Bexley. As such she undoubtedly deserves recognition for the work she has undertaken to date, and for her outstanding contribution to our future generation.

Philip's memorial school in Africa

Philip in action

Tributes to Philip

Life is not about how long we live on this earth, but what we achieve while we are here. Some people live a long life, and don't achieve very much. Others live a short life, yet their legacy lives on forever.

—Bishop Clement Amankwah-Asihene

Benjamin

There is so much to say about Philip. First and foremost, Philip was my little brother; and he was the best I could have asked for.

I met Philip at our family church, Wellspring Pentecostal, when he was about 5 years old. At that time, my family were new to the church, whereas Philip and Auntie Juliet were already attenders. We all didn't know it then, or perhaps we weren't entirely sure; but we all would become very close from that moment on, particularly Philip and I.

I don't know the year and date that our brotherhood status was officially established, but I like to think it was immediate. Before I knew it, I wasn't just seeing Philip every weekend at Church like the rest of the kids, but everywhere other than in church. I was seeing him at my house. And not just at my house, but also in my room, on my PlayStation, in my bed, at family dinners, Easters, Christmases, Mothers Days, family holidays, all of which involved eating our food. The boy could eat, and if it wasn't clear before, these things definitely qualified him for brother status.

Looking back, there are plenty of fond memories that I have of Philip. I will never forget Philip's haircuts and the infamous crop circles that were shaved into his hair. All I knew at the time was that no little brother of mine was going to remain my little brother with a haircut like that. Yes, I loved him no matter what, but that wasn't the point. My having a little brother meant that he had to have style, and though I'm sure Juliet thought his hair was very stylish, it was my responsibility to show both Philip and his mum the light. I guess this was one of the first lessons I can recall teaching Philip – that your image matters. It wasn't that Philip's appearance was untidy or not presentable. I just wanted him to be cool, moreover, I wanted everyone else to think he was cool. So the crop circles were dropped and 'waves' brought in.

Now, the 'waves' were an important lesson, and definitely, a big brother inspired motive. Philip was given precise instructions on how to look after his hair. As well as this being an upgrade for him, this was also an opportunity for me to see how well he would listen and heed my wise teachings. Philip could only buy as follows: Sporting waves hair pomade, the (RED TIN) Dax, or Lusters 360 S-curl pomade. He then was required to purchase a doo rag, or in his case, borrow his mum's stockings, and then further acquire a medium thistle hairbrush. Once he had these, the wave grooming process could begin. After I had gone through the technique for brushing with him numerous times, I was happy to say that it eventually sank in.

Philip had passed his first younger brother test. Whenever he came round he had all his wave utensils, and would sort his hair out himself without my help before going to bed. At a point, his waves were better than mine, and that was a big brother proud moment. In this simple act of brushing hair, Philip showed commitment to this little task and ended up mastering it. These weren't just steps to being cool, but insight into his character and nature.

After the waves came the clothes. Now, neither Philip nor I was financially independent at the time, so the struggles he faced when trying to ask his mum for new clothes, I also faced. I'd give Philip a list of items to ask his mum for, and would feel better knowing that if I couldn't get them, at least one of us could. I guess the clothes weren't just another factor towards making Philip look cool, or making him stand out, it was more than that. It was more so that, wherever he went, he would be a reflection of me.

Every older brother wants their younger one to be kitted out, because we know wherever they go and whoever they meet, in some small way they represent us. Almost like how sons are meant to be representations of their fathers, Philip represented me. Thinking about it, it wasn't just Philip that represented me, I also represented him. As much as it was his mission to carry out little brother training to become the best little brother, it was my responsibility to maintain the image of what a big brother could be. If Philip had a problem I had no choice but to go and help, if he was getting into a fight, I would have had no choice but to intervene, and if he didn't have a toothbrush, socks, jacket, jeans, game or hairbrush, it was my responsibility to provide it. My image to others wasn't just important because I thought so, but it was all the more important, because it was Philip's perception of me, and his portrayal of me unto others, which is what really mattered.

After image training came strength training— my favourite one. Strength training was fun. It would consist of play-fighting and playing on the PlayStation for endless amounts of hours a day. Believe it or not, these two exercises taught Philip a lot. They were physical and mental conditioning combined.

From when he was small and started sleeping over my house, Philip's strength training went into full effect. Now if I'm honest, Philip wasn't one for play-fighting. As a matter of fact, he would be the first to interject when Lydia and I were fighting. He would tell us to stop. However, I did give him a choice. I was determined to get his 'cry baby' nature out of him. Philip would cry for everything. If he weren't getting his own way, he'd cry. If he were threatened with a smack, he'd start crying straight away, instead of thinking of a solution to avoid getting one.

I just kept imagining him in the playground, or in the park, then someone coming over to him and pushing him, and instead of doing anything about it, he'd just cry. This would not do. So I would grab him and throw him on the bed, tell him to get back up, and then push him back on the bed again, and if he got hit too hard he would have to 'firm it'. Naturally, as you can guess, after about the second push and a medium punch, Philip would start crying, and depending on how severe or loud it was, a lot of our training sessions were cut short.

I showed Philip how to do press ups, and showed him how to punch properly, and eventually, the serial crying stopped. I'm not sure if it was the repetitive, 'shut up, Philip,' 'shush, Philip,' or 'Philip you're just a cry baby,' that Lydia and I said all too often, that stopped his crying, but it stopped nonetheless.

I will never forget playing Dragon Ball Z with him. Oh, Lord! I don't think I was even ready for those tears or that lesson, but this game definitely helped develop Philip's winning mentality. At the time, I was much more proficient in playing PlayStation than Philip was. I had been raised on fighting games, and had gone through similar training sessions from my older cousins. I used to let Philip beat me a couple of times in the first few rounds, and I remember how happy he used to get. Then, just when he was feeling on top, I would really start to play, and, yes, you guessed it; tears, lots of tears. But that didn't stop me from thrashing him, because this was all part of my training Philip. I wanted him to overcome the tears and play as hard as he could, and credit where it was due, Philip would never give up. Most boys his age would have cried and then dropped the control, but not Philip. He would cry through the games, but keep on playing. He didn't know it, but he was subconsciously building up his mental strength, or perhaps it was strength that he already had, but was unlocking.

The more we played the better he became. The matches became so intense. That's when I really started to enjoy them, and as I expected he eventually started to beat me – regularly, too. Sometimes, something as simple as playing a game can teach you a lot, and reveal a lot about a person. When I look back at those times playing against Philip, even though he cried, he never once got angry. Even if he was frustrated, he restrained himself, and carried on playing graciously. And thinking about it, these were traits of his maturity. His non-confrontational attitude and his humility when playing games were also examples of strength, ones that I hadn't really acknowledged or thought about. Not once did Philip boast about winning a game.

It was instances like these that made me realise, it wasn't just about making him physically stronger, or making sure he had the best hair and clothes. It was about helping him achieve a balance. Yes, I wanted him to be tough mentally and physically, and be resilient to whatever came his way, but there was more to being a big brother than getting him to focus on those things alone. It was about making sure that his roots were solid. That those same roots that had been planted in him by his mother, were still being nurtured and watered by God.

However, as much as that realisation became apparent to me, I think that through Philip's own growth and maturity, he managed to achieve that balance much earlier than I anticipated. Thinking back, it was clear that the attributes that contributed to this balance were all blessings from God.

Philip loved God from a young age, and it was because he loved God first, and cherished his mum above all others, that I knew he would become a great man; and I had looked forward to watching him grow and develop in himself in God.

Nothing could have prepared me for Philip's death, and there are some days where it doesn't feel like he is gone at all. Sometimes I still struggle with God's choice to take him at such a young age. I wonder what the future might have held if he were still here with us. Nonetheless, he was called home, and my assurance of that is through my faith and trust in God. The same faith Philip shared. I could talk about all the things Philip might have and would have accomplished if he were still here, and many others would also testify to this. He was smart, handsome and of course extremely athletic. However, despite these things, I have come to realise that a mark of true exceptionality is that of a person who carries on accomplishing even after they have left us. I have witnessed transformation in the lives of young people, schools, churches and communities, all because of Philip's passing; and his legacy lives on.

The PL9 Foundation has been one of the most influential and inspiring ideas to come out of it all. The foundation has worked directly with young people, tackling some hard-hitting issues that affect teenagers today. What makes it so special is that most of the teenagers that first attended were Philip's friends. Some of them struggled to come to terms with Philip's passing and were in need of encouragement, and mentorship. I was fortunate enough to have been invited by Juliet to speak to these young people directly. It was comforting because I knew I wasn't the only one who felt the way I did. It was a platform to engage and talk to them about Philip and about situations that they were facing within their own lives. I think that Philip's death caused them to stop and reflect on where they were in their own lives, and question the direction in which they were heading. By contributing my own experiences and stepping into a mentorship role, I became an ambassador for Philip and for God in serving the younger generation. The PL9 foundation targeted a lot of the issues with a God-centred approach, which was exactly where Philip and myself were coming from; so it provided a healthy balance for these young people's lives. When I think about it now, although my little brother had to leave, what I ended up with instead was a whole new family of brothers and sisters, all of whom I am greatly thankful for.

Philip's death brought life and light into all of these things. It was not by chance that Philip was a Christian, he was hand-picked by God to do what God had intended him to do. These accomplishments are a reflection of his walk and a testament to his faith. It is that same faith in God that redeems the heart of men. It can bring peace to a wounded spirit and remedy a broken heart even in the most unpredicted, unforeseen and unprepared of times.

Whoever reads this should take note of how Philip lived his life. His legacy will live forever through me, through his family and friends, and through the people his death has touched.

I miss my little brother, but I say to myself, and to all who know his God; we shall see him again!

KRISTY

Philip Lamin, my brother who left me very early. He lived a short but fulfilling life and left a long legacy for us to remember him by. The date, 5th of February 2013, will never leave my mind, as it is the day we all lost a son, brother, friend and just simply, someone so special. The emphasis of Philip 'living a short life, but leaving a long legacy' still echoes in my mind to this very day. Indeed it proves that it's not so much about the length of your years, but more about the worth and impact of your years on earth.

Philip and I attended the same church where I first encountered him with his mum, Auntie Juliet. Philip was also one of my brother's best friends, so he was always in my life. Philip spent plenty of time in my house, played on the same football team as my brother, and stayed over at my house on numerous occasions. Through this, we developed a strong friendship and a sibling-like relationship with one another. He was always at my house with my brother and his other friends; always sending me to buy food for him or always finishing my mum's Jollof Rice – he was famous in my house for always finishing the Jollof Rice!

Philip loved his food. I strongly remember one occasion where my brother, Philip and I baked some cookies that did not turn out as we planned—it was hilarious! He even informed me about several occasions where he 'had my back' when I was not around. Philip was such a pleasant, polite and handsome young man—my family loved him, he was always welcome over.

When Philip touched a football, you knew he was destined to be a footballer. You would always see Philip in a different light whenever he engaged with the ball—whether it was in the football cage by my house, playing a match for our church football team or an actual league team game. On the pitch, he stood out as a star and leader of men; his skills were different and his approach and swagger could never really be matched on the pitch.

On the 5th of February 2013, around 5pm, my mum received a call from my brother who was out with Philip and all their friends ('the batch' as they were called) saying that Philip had collapsed while doing what he loved best, playing football. I remember being really panicky. I remember hurriedly rushing to my phone and buzzing off Philip's phone on Blackberry Messenger to check if he was okay, but of course, there was no reply.

I was eventually told Philip was fine, so continued with my normal evening routine (not knowing that he had probably passed away already). Despite being told he was fine, my dad and auntie rushed to Queen Elizabeth Hospital to meet my brother and everyone else who went with Philip to the hospital. A while passed and then I heard screams outside the front door—it was my mum who had just received a phone call, and it came to my realisation that Philip was no longer with us.

Philip meant so much to us. My mum, little sister and I then rushed to the hospital, I remember being in my pyjamas, slippers and carrying a napkin to cushion my tears. I remember arriving at the hospital and witnessing Philip in such a peaceful state, just lying there; he had gone to be with the Lord.

After Philip's death, I was so lost. How could someone so fit, young and healthy lose their life so unexpectedly? It is almost impossible to explain how unexpected this passing was. I asked myself why God had taken Auntie Juliet's only son—her only child—knowing they were both so strong in their walk with Christ. As a young Christian, I found it so hard to gather up all my thoughts and produce an answer. I had never lost anybody so close to me before—this was the first time. Philip's passing would run through my mind 24/7. The Saturday of that week, my youth church and I went to go and visit Auntie Juliet in her home. Although distraught, we left full of courage and knowing that God would forever be glorified and Philip's legacy would still live on.

We arrived at the house and found Auntie Juliet seated with her relatives, wearing one of Philip's football shirts. I'll be honest with you, I have never met anybody so strong; Auntie's courage, strength and warm embrace that day is a memory that I will never forget. We went upstairs into Philip's room, exchanging reminiscences of Philip and then sang songs including '*My Soul Magnifies the Lord*' - another memory that I will never forget. I couldn't believe how tough Auntie Juliet was being, as I could never imagine myself in such a situation. Despite her loss, Auntie insisted on remaining true to Almighty God and as time passed, we all came together believing that God's time is not our time and He knew what He was doing.

Philip's funeral brought together a vast number of people reflecting on how much Philip was adored and how he would forever be missed. Personally, I found it very hard to control my emotions that day, but seeing Philip in such a different state really affected me. From that day, I knew I had to remain strong and make both Philip and Auntie Juliet proud. His passing created an impact on those close to him and even those who were not so close to him. On the 8th of March 2013, Philip's life was truly celebrated regardless of all the hurt. In the midst of it all, God remained faithful and to this day remains the same. Through his passing, many even dedicated themselves to God or grew closer to Him.

Philip's passing did not only bring dreadful sorrow, it formed a new family of the people that cared dearly about Philip. Auntie Juliet succeeded in her endeavours of forming a forum in the name of Philip, which was named 'PL9'. This was a forum of young people who were close to Philip and others who were invited along. In PL9, we came together to discuss topical issues affecting our generation. Many different speakers have attended these forums to enlighten us and left a great impact on us—this was all through the passing of Philip Lamin. Some of the highlights of the PL9 forum have been the annual Christmas Party and the Talent Showcase, which brought together gospel artistes from across London.

Auntie Juliet has accomplished many different things over the 2 years after the passing of our beloved brother Philip, and I am assured that the Lord has greater things planned for her. Auntie lost a son but became a mother to many different people on the 5th of February 2013. Through PL9, I have made many friendships with people I might never have met. Philip's passing also opened a door for me to have an opportunity to complete a week's work experience with the Mayor of Greenwich in 2014. As mentioned before, Auntie Juliet was led by God to complete many different accomplishments after her son's passing and I was presented with this unique opportunity, from which I benefitted greatly.

To this day it still affects me, I still have unanswered questions, but God, day by day, is opening my mind to why he does certain things. Trust Him.

Even in your passing Philip, you continue to open doors for people and present them with new opportunities. You'll be celebrated for-ever, Philip! The love of God endures forever.

DEL

Philip was like a grandson to me—a boy to be proud of. His passion for football knew no bounds. Philip and his Mum, Juliet (our spir-itual daughter), lived on a road adjacent to ours. The roads terminated at Franks Park where there was a football/basketball com-pound. Sometimes I would leave my house to walk our dog at 7am, and could hear the bouncing of a ball on the tarmac some 100 yards away, and yes, it was Philip practising his football skills, come rain or shine. Philip was always polite and would say 'Good morn-ing Pastor Del.'

Philip and Juliet attended our church where I was Pastor in 2002 when Philip was small and we connected with them straight away.

I remember him reciting the whole of Psalm 91 to our congregation when he was about 7 years old!

When I received an answer phone message one bitterly cold February afternoon from Juliet, I could sense panic in her voice as she said that Philip had fallen on the football pitch, and that we should pray. She was making her way to the hospital, as he'd been rushed there. Philip was young and athletic and in top physical condition, so my wife, Carol, and I assumed he'd simply fainted due to the cold. Then we rang Juliet, realised the seriousness of his situation and rushed to the Queen Elizabeth hospital to find that he was lying dead on a trolley bed. He had a tube down his throat and it was obvious everything had been done to resuscitate him, to no avail.

Immediately we began to pray. Jesus told his disciples to heal the sick, raise the dead, cleanse those who have leprosy, drive out demons and it's a clear mandate to us today. I asked the nurse if we could have a room to pray and she said that it wasn't hospital policy—however, when Carol and Juliet and myself, and Len Randall our youth pastor began passionately and fervently storming heaven with our prayer, they changed their minds and ushered us into a children's ward which was not being used. Oh, how we prayed with no doubt in our hearts that God could, and would, raise Philip from the dead! We prayed for hours, and others joined us. I remember the attending Police officers looking on in bewilderment. Philip would be raised.

Eventually, we were asked to leave but a Christian nurse invited us back to the mortuary the following morning, and we held a praise and worship meeting with several Pastors present including Pastor Frank Payne. Some of Philip's friends from Bexleyheath Academy arrived and showed such courage. However, I asked all those without the faith for Philip to be raised to leave the room and we pressed on, undaunted. Then came an overriding sense of peace and I knew, at that point, that Philip was remaining in glory with the Lord and not returning. We gradually said our goodbyes and left with heavy hearts.

The very next day Juliet called to say that the students at the academy were traumatised and stunned by all that had taken place, and she asked if I could attend as they'd been ushered into an assembly room. Typically, Juliet was thinking of their welfare before her own. When we arrived, I felt helpless as 20 to 30 young people sat around the table with me in silence. Len arrived later, as did Pastor Frank. I asked the Holy Spirit to give me something to say when I noticed a football coach clasping a football. I asked for the ball and said to the young people:

'You haven't had a chance to say goodbye to your friend—if you'd known what was going to happen what would you have said to him? This is your chance right now. You are going to pass the ball to one another, and as you receive it, speak about your feelings for him, and don't hold back.'

We began passing the ball and the outpouring was incredible. Tears and laughter –jokes and innuendo—it was so therapeutic. Most of the girls had had a crush on him as Philip was handsome, or 'fit' as they would say. One girl said that Philip had had a dream about her and it was quite expressive and everyone laughed as he obviously had a bit of a 'crush' on her. Another student said that Philip would playfully hit him about the head as he passed him in the corridor and he never got his own back. Others just said how much they'd loved him and said their goodbyes in their own unique way. It was very touching and evident that he'd made a deep impression on all of them, and that his faith had shone through.

Since then, the outpouring of love and support for Juliet, for one another and from teachers at the Academy; and the encouragement of the wonderful Principal, Carl Wakefield, has been astonishing. I recently interviewed Juliet for Revelation TV, and the response has been amazing. I'm so proud of Juliet, and as Police Chaplain of the Borough, I have helped facilitate meetings between our Borough Commander and the young people where they have advised the Police on the matter of their 'Stop and Search' powers and impressed us all with their creative ideas and eloquence. Respect for the Police has grown and the respect is mutual.

Romans 8:28 (NIV) says, *'In all things God works for the good of those who love Him.'* Never have I witnessed the truth in a passage of scripture as I have through our loss of Philip. But as Juliet says, 'there must be a formidable football team in heaven and Philip is part of it!'

Philip's legacy lives on, and I'm sure there will be many more doors of opportunity that will open through PL9 and other initiatives, all as a result of Philip's life, because the truth is that we *will* see him again one day, and he's more alive than ever and enjoying heaven.

KEVIN

Philip Lamin, 'a young man who has lived a short earthly life but has left a long legacy'. Those were the words of my Bishop, Bishop Clement Amankwah-Asihene on 8th March 2013, during the funeral service of Philip, which brought together over 1,000 people, both young and old. Those words still ring true and clear in my ears today, and emphasise that the length of one's life doesn't matter so much, but the impact it makes does.

My first encounter with Philip was in the summer of 2009 during our annual church youth camp meeting. As we assembled in the car park ready to board the coach, I introduced myself to Philip as a youth leader and that if he needed anything he could come to me. A twelve-year-old boy at the time, he was polite and pleasant like most boys his age, but then he said something that struck me,

'The waves in my hair are better than yours.'

I paused for a second then burst into laughter. I honestly couldn't believe how cheeky he was being, but I immediately warmed to him. Over the course of the following three days, I watched him closely as we went through various activities and lessons at the camp meeting. He participated without any issues and gelled with the young boys instantly; boys who would become brothers in the years that followed.

On the second evening of the camp, after service, we (the boys) changed into our football kit and went out to the nearby field for a kick about. That evening I saw Philip in a different light; although it was a friendly game, he stood out. He stood out as a leader, one whose passion, dedication and, most importantly, skill couldn't be matched by anyone on the pitch. I vividly recall him running effortlessly throughout the entire game and virtually having to be marched off the pitch as it was bedtime; getting those boys up in the morning was always a nightmare. Camp finished, we returned to London, and I continued to see Philip; most often at our weekly youth services, purposely organised to equip and empower young people to carry the gospel to their community. With time, Philip's football commitments meant that he couldn't be at every service, but I wasn't too worried because I knew that, in Auntie Juliet, he had a mother whose faith and knowledge of the word of God was exceptional. I knew that he would never forget his God.

On the 5th February 2013, around 8pm in the evening, having returned from work, I received a call from one of my youth members. I picked up the phone to hear uncontrollable crying and the statement 'Kevin, Philip is dead!'

I was confused and didn't really understand, so I asked, 'What do you mean? Philip who?' Philip Lamin was the last person that came to mind; he was too young, too fit, he was a footballer, it couldn't be him.

Then the confirmation came, 'Philip Lamin; Auntie Juliet's son.'

I couldn't speak; I was stunned and shocked. My thoughts immediately turned to the grieving mother; she had lost her only son; her only child. As the hours passed that evening, my phone was flooded with calls and texts from confused and distraught young people, asking why and how God could allow this to happen. The hardest thing was explaining to them that, although our friend and brother was no more, God was, is and forever will be sovereign and loving.

The Saturday of that week was even harder; having to come face to face with my youth for the first time since Philip's passing. To be honest I didn't know how to deal with it; what to say or what to do. After a time of praise and worship, I took to the pulpit. Looking into the faces of my brothers and sisters, I could see 30 to 40 lost and hurting young people. Feeling pain myself, having lost a close family friend just weeks before, I became angry and told them that 'Philip's passing must show us all that life is short and you must devote yourself wholly to God.' After I had ranted for a few minutes, they stared at me blankly, and I realised that comforting these youth couldn't be done in my own strength, so we turned to God. That afternoon for about 15 to 20 minutes, we prayed in the spirit and the atmosphere changed for good. As we left church that afternoon to go to Philip's' home to visit Auntie Juliet, we left empowered and determined that God's work would still go on, and if anything, it would go on to honour our brother.

Upon entering the house, we found Auntie Juliet sitting down with some relatives, wearing Philip's school football shirt; an image that will stay with me forever. Her embrace that day was so tight, but her courage was amazing. As we sat in Philip's room praying and singing *'My soul magnify the Lord and my spirit praise his name'*, I couldn't help but think of what my own mother would do in Auntie Juliet's shoes. The circumstances were truly devastating but she still chose to praise and give thanks to God.

The weeks passed, and we all put our minds and efforts together to ensure that Philip was given a befitting farewell. I was given the singular honour of reading out a tribute to the congregation on behalf of my youth; an incredibly difficult task to carry out without losing my composure. The scenes of his school friends scrambling to carry his coffin out to the hearse for his final journey spoke powerfully of a young man who was and is still loved by all who encountered him.

It came to light during the funeral service that Philip's favourite portion of scripture was Psalm 91, a chapter which in verse 2 says, *'I will say of the Lord 'He is my refuge and my fortress; my God in Him I will trust.'* (NKJV) That's all we could do after the events of 5th February 2013; trust in God. Auntie Juliet has personified Psalm 91:2 from that day till date in all her actions, speech and faith.

Philip's passing had a huge impact on the youth group, on those who were close and not so close to him. Personally, it had an impact on my leadership and understanding of how to deal with difficult times, but in the midst of it all, God has been glorified, for we are convinced that our brother rests peacefully in the bosom of his Maker. Many came to know God after Philip left us, some even recommitted themselves to God, and in that sense, Philip's loss came as a wake-up call to us all.

In the two years after the burial of our brother Philip, Auntie Juliet has accomplished some amazing feats, including the establishment of the PL9 Forum; a forum for young people to come together and discuss topical issues affecting their age groups and society. I've been privileged to be able to impact and speak into the lives of people through the forum, and I'm assured that greater things lie in store. Auntie Juliet has become a mother to many people in the last 2 years and has been used by God to bless people in diverse ways. In her, we have 'the soil that bore Philip's seed', a simply incredible woman. She has also made incredible efforts to spread the worrying facts regarding heart conditions, which are unknown to many of us. Through sheer determination and driven by the legacy of Philip, her message has spread across the borough and city, and it's only a matter of time before she's sitting at No. 10 Downing Street pushing for change.

I'm honoured to have been asked to contribute to the writing of this book and pray that it will be a blessing to whoever picks it up to read. Young people are so precious in the sight of God and he is yearning that we give ourselves to be used by him for the expansion of his kingdom. Ecclesiastes 12: 1 (NIV) reminds us to '*Remember [our] creator in the*

days of [our] youth, before the days of trou-
ble come...' (writer's words in parenthesis)
Philip knew God in the days of his youth and
had a relationship with him, so we can con-
fidently say that he is with Him. I personally
believe that Philip accomplished his God-giv-
en mission and his impact will be felt for gen-
erations to come through his mother, family
and friends. Although his loss was painful,
and still is, Philip has run his race, he can run
no more this earthly race, so it is up to us to
continue and ensure that his legacy lives on.

'Short life, long legacy'. Philip Lamin, rest in
perfect peace.

EMMANUEL

Philip Lamin, a name that, even till today,
speaks volumes in my life. This boy, this
friend, this brother is someone I have known
from as early as it is possible to remember. As
a twin myself, I have one biological brother,
but he made us a trio, a third leg on which we
both stood.

When we were younger there were times we
lived together. We met each other, according

to our parents, through a play club my brother and I attended after school every day. Our parents became friends through our friendship. He made us triplets, although the irony is that Philip was a year younger than us. Our great bond revolved around football, which we always played together. Funny enough, he and my brother were better than me at the sport, as my focus as a child was more on Art, and I had a keen interest in books and reading.

There were many great moments that I recall having with Philip, and they are priceless to me. I distinctively remember us watching *Rush Hour* and *Rush Hour 2* with Philip when he lived in Welling. We did this while eating some paprika potato chips. Honestly, to this day, whenever I watch those films, I can hear our laughter together echoing in my mind, and more distinctively, his laughter. He had a very abstract laugh as far as I can remember.

I also remember us watching our favourite programme , *Dragon Ball Z*, together, where we used to mimic the characters and fight each other in my living room as if we were the characters. We were almost obsessed with the show and got our parents to buy us the video games, which we never stopped playing as we competed against each other to see who was best at the game. We never really had a dull moment together. We were family and we will always be family. Philip is among the selected few childhood friends who have never left my life, even until today, and whom I regard to be my family.

Philip loved his football. Arsenal was his team and he almost idolised Thierry Henry because of this. It was very much two against one, as my twin also supported Arsenal whereas I supported Manchester United. Nevertheless, we loved each other.

Philip was a happy soul, sometimes a cry-baby, as he would start crying as soon as he got into some trouble. I do have to say we were quite mischievous together. He was, even if I didn't realise it at the time, a positive influence in my life. He taught me always to stay positive, no matter what, and to keep going until you can go no further, because that was the type of person he was. He never gave up.

Philip's death was sudden and was much unexpected. It hit hard, and even today, I am still trying to come to terms with it. It was a normal day in February, 5th February 2013, to be precise. Philip was a passionate footballer who played regularly. He was good at football and knew that he was beginning to be really successful. He had the possibility of a great future in this field, and was on the verge of being signed by Fulham Football Club. That day in February, Philip was playing at the nearby Goals Soccer Centre, next to Bexleyheath Academy, where he had played on many occasions. The game was going well. He had just scored a goal. There were the usual celebrations; it was just a friendly game so spirits were high.

But the story is a tragic one, seconds after scoring that goal, Philip collapsed on the pitch. Help was urgently called for by his friends, but unfortunately, by the time the ambulance got to him it was too late, and

Philip died on that pitch at the age of just 16. That was his last goal.

We lost a brother and friend. His mum lost her only son. As you can imagine, we, his friends, were in disarray and shocked, as Philip never showed any signs of this ever happening to him. The doctors found the cause of his sudden death was cardiac arrest. He and we had no knowledge of him having any cardiac related issues beforehand, as is the case for many young people with the same story. As far as we knew, he was a healthy young boy.

We learned later that had there been a defibrillator available, it is possible that Philip would have been saved. If he was attended to immediately with this piece of equipment, he could still be with us today. If he had been screened routinely, any underlying heart problems could have been detected. But Philip's life was gone in such a short moment.

He was known for his lovable character and personality and was known and loved by many. Philip was like a brother to me, one whom I grew up with; he helped me become who I am today. I still grieve his death, even today, and he will forever be in my heart.

After he died, I really found it hard in school, and my family were distraught. We just couldn't believe it. He was gone. Sometime after the funeral, Philip's Mum (Juliet Lamin) or as I know her, Auntie Juliet, had a conversation with me about leadership, and she said she always saw the qualities of a leader in me from since I was young. At first, I thought this was absurd, as I couldn't really see these qualities within myself.

However, she then mentioned she wanted to start this youth group to bring awareness of cardiac risk in the young and to help the general youth community in our local area. She was driven. She requested that I be the leader of this group. At first, I was very hesitant, as I hadn't taken on a role of such responsibility before in my life, as I always like to just coast by. But she believed in me and saw something in me that I was yet to see within myself. Funny enough, Philip did, too.

I had an experience one night that will never leave me for the rest of my life, I was sleeping and dreaming as I usually do, and I was dreaming about me, Sam and Philip playing video games as we usually did. It felt so real, but it was a dream. In my dream, I didn't realise that Philip was gone from our world, and everything was normal. Then randomly, Philip touched me and it all came to me, the fact that he was dead and no longer with us, the fact that this was a dream, and what I needed to do.

Philip appeared to me in that dream to confirm to me that I was ready and good enough to be this leader. That dream gave me the confidence I needed, and that is why I chose to work with his mother, Juliet Lamin, to start a youth forum working to raise awareness of Cardiac Risk in the young, to educate the young in the local community about cardiac risks. We have worked to teach people how to get their hearts checked at their local GP surgery, as well as how to cope with life as someone with cardiac-related issues. Fundraising events have been held to raise the money to provide defibrillators for local organisations, so that there is equipment available, just in case.

Having experienced first-hand what happened with Philip, we at PL9 do not want anything like this to happen to anyone else in the community and in the world. No mother should go through the pain of losing her son; young people should not have to experience the loss of valued friends.

Through PL9 I have successfully placed defibrillators in many schools across my local community, met and spoken to people I would have otherwise never met, and I have become a stronger person because of it. Before PL9, I was the guy who would stand in the back while presentations are going on, or be the guy who hides in the corner when he hears the word 'speech'. But now, I regard myself as a good public speaker. Through PL9 I have had to speak to a variety of audiences, it has therefore improved my presentational skills, my confidence and my ability to speak to people.

I am very grateful for PL9 as it has been a platform for me to higher stages. As a leader, I have brought my people a long way and made them not only to be aware of cardiac risks in the young but educated them to follow in my footsteps and educate those around them, as the world needs to know that 12 young people die each week from cardiac-related issues.

Just take that in. For me, that is 12 way too many.

PL9 stands for Philip Lamin and the number 9 was Philip's number on his football shirt. The organisation is not only about educating people on cardiac risks among the young, but making a difference in the youth community. The youth forum's intentions were not only to educate but to listen to the concerns of young people. Its goal is to Listen, Encourage and Develop (L.E.A.D). We are a team of a mixture of youths with some adult supervision, whereby the youth like me run this forum. I am designated as the leader but, essentially, we are run by the youth to give to the youth.

Also, the forum is to encourage young people to actively engage in open group discussions, which will provide them with positive influences, focus structures and new experiences to help both confidence and team building.

We are bringing young people from a variety of backgrounds and cultures together, initially on a weekly basis, in a safe and secure environment with the aim of encouraging creative thought, cultural awareness, and broadening their horizons by equipping them with new life skills that they can use for personal development and betterment.

We are PL9.

MRS NINA NDUBUISI

5th February 2013

I will never forget the evening of the 5th of February 2013. I still feel goose bumps erupting all over me each time I cast my mind back to that night.

My husband and I were sitting in our living room, and our daughter Nicole, came to us, sobbing heavily, with tears running down her face. She sat down in the chair opposite without saying a word, and we had to turn the volume of the television down to give her the attention she needed. She managed to get herself together and blurted out;

'I think my friend has died.'

Me: 'Which friend?'

Nicole: 'Philip.'

Me: 'Which Philip?'

Nicole: 'Philip from my school.'

Me: 'What happened to him?'

Nicole: 'They said his heart stopped.'

Me: 'What do you mean his heart stopped?'

My husband and I looked at each other and Nicole started crying hysterically again. I found myself going over to her and hugging her. I had to ask her which Philip she was referring to, as I knew she had two friends called Philip. She told me 'Philip Lamin'.

I asked her to tell us what she meant by, 'I think my friend has died.' She then told me how she had read it on Facebook and had tried to contact the person that posted it, but their phone was switched off. I asked her if she had tried to contact Philip, and she said his phone was switched off as well.

I tried as much as I could to console her and told her that it must just be a joke. After all, we know how kids play expensive jokes all the time and post them on Facebook. My husband and I managed to console her, we prayed together as a family and sent her to bed.

The following morning, I went into her room to wake her and saw she was wide awake, her eyes were red and swollen from crying. She had not slept at all. In my heart, I still believed that Philip was not dead and that it was just an expensive joke that the kids were playing. We said our morning prayers as a family and I sent Nicole to school with strict instructions to phone me immediately she got to school.

My eyes were fixated on the clock as I waited for the school office to open, as I needed to speak to the school and hear it from them. I eventually got through to them but was told that they could not give me any information.

Nicole finally contacted me and told me that it was true, and that she was at the bus stop with a group of others and that they were going to the hospital to the mortuary. I found myself screaming down the phone at her asking,

'Mortuary? What do you mean you are going to the mortuary?'

She replied, 'We are going to the mortuary to see Philip?'

Me – 'What's Philip doing in the mortuary?'

At this point, Nicole started crying, then I started hearing the other kids in the background crying. That's when it eventually dawned on me that Philip had 'gone'.

I am not sure how I managed to get on with work that day, as my heart was heavy with sadness and grief. I was so concerned for the children who had lost a beloved, most of who would be dealing with the death of a close one for the first time. My heart was especially heavy for the parents of Philip. At this time,

I had never met Juliet Lamin, neither was I aware that Philip was an only child.

I found myself clock-watching that day, something that I hardly ever do, seeing as I love my job so much. I found myself doing this, as I needed to get out and go and be with my daughter and accompany her to visit Philip's mum.

When I got home that day, my house was packed with some of the girls from Bexleyheath Academy school. They were all subdued with puffy eyes. I sat with them and asked them to tell me what had happened. They narrated their own version of events – how Philip had been playing football after school and had collapsed on the pitch after scoring a goal, and that he died immediately in the arms of his best friend, Miljan.

I took a deep breath and composed myself, as I felt my eyes welling up with tears, but I knew I needed to be strong for these kids and also for Philip's mum (although I was still yet to meet her). I went to my room and said a quick prayer asking God to send me the wisdom and strength I would need to embark on this journey. Little did I know that I was going to meet someone whom the Holy Spirit had already filled with strength, and who was going to be a source of strength and inspiration to all of us—Juliet Lamin.

When I walked into Juliet's house on the 6th of February 2013, in true African fashion, the house was packed with people singing uplifting Christian songs. I saw a few familiar faces and more kids from Bexleyheath Academy, some I recognised and some I had never met. Unbeknown to me, I was going to become part of these kids' lives over the next few months.

I went over to one lady and asked her to show me Philip's mum. She pointed her out to me, and as my eyes fell on her I was shocked. I had expected to see a woman crying or wailing in the midst of all the chaos, but what I saw was a sight that has remained with me.

I saw a small young lady with golden dreadlocks, wearing a yellow football shirt, dancing to the Christians songs in the middle of the room. She had her eyes closed and was most likely meditating within herself. I looked back at the lady who had pointed me in the direction to confirm whether that was actually Philip's mum, and she nodded. I went over to her and hugged her as tightly as I could. As I held her, I felt a song burst out of my mouth;

Hear my cry, O Lord, attend unto my prayer

From the end of the earth, will I cry unto thee

And when my heart is overwhelmed,

Lead me to the rock

That is higher than I,

That is higher than I.

Everyone in the room joined me in singing. At this point, I felt Juliet try to loosen herself from my embrace to see who this person was that was holding her so tightly, but I did not want to let her go, because at this point I was unable to control my tears any longer, and I did not want her to see me crying. I then started another chorus:

It is to you I give the glory.

It is to you I give the praise

For you have done so much for me and I will bless your holy name

It is to you Holy Father, no one like you

And I will bless your name, bless your name

And I will bless your name forever more.

At this point, I let go of Juliet and she looked at me. Obviously, she could not identify me, as we had never met before. At this point, my tears were flowing, and I felt Juliet embrace and pat me on the back as though she was telling me, 'It's alright. It is well. Philip is in a better place.'

The choruses died down and we all sat down. I went and sat with the kids and did my best to try and console them, as they had all broken down again. I looked over at Juliet and people were trying to make small talk with her. I then watched her stand up from her seat and heard her say 'let me go and talk to the kids.'

I watched her walk towards our direction and continued to watch her, as she sat on the floor with her legs crossed in front of the girls. The boys were around, but they had all gone up to Philip's room. I listened to her console the girls. I heard her telling them not to cry anymore, but to be happy that Philip is now in a better place.

I could feel myself becoming angry at this point. I kept asking myself, *What manner of woman is this?*

It wasn't yet 48 hours Philip had 'gone', and instead of her rolling on the ground, screaming and shouting and tearing her clothes like a mad person, she was here sitting on the floor consoling others and telling them that her son, her only child, the only fruit that had germinated from her womb had gone to a 'better place'.

Which kind of 'better place' was this she was talking about? What place was she describing that could be better than being at home with his mum, with his friends and with all others who loved and cherished him? Here she was, telling them that they should not cry, and that she was going to be here for them throughout. Little did I know that this was just the beginning of my relationship with a remarkable, inspirational and phenomenal woman.

As days rolled into weeks, and it became clear, although still hard to digest, that Philip Lamin was well and truly gone and never coming back, I found myself visiting Juliet Lamin on a daily basis. Plans for the funeral were well and truly underway; the kids were able to divert their minds by raising funds for the funeral.

At this point, the flow of 'visitors' had started to dwindle, although the kids' presence remained constant in Juliet's house. One day I called Juliet to find out how she was doing, and she told me that she was about to go into the kitchen to cook chicken and rice for the kids as they were all coming to her house after school. I could feel that sense of 'ungodly' anger begin to rise within me again, but, thankfully, God spoke to me and assured me that what Juliet was doing was her way of dealing with her grief, and I should try not to be angry, but that I should just support Juliet in whatever way I could as she embraced the kids.

It wasn't until a few days later that Juliet told me that she had seen Philip in a dream and that he had asked her to take care of his friends and take them as her own children.

It's been two years now since Philip left us. I was one of the 'visitors', but, thankfully, I ended up as one of the constant 'visitors' who stayed in Juliet's life.

I have found Juliet very inspirational. I have watched her take a negative situation and turn it into a positive. I have watched her change lives amongst the teenagers; I have watched her strengthen the relationships within the community. I have watched her empower schools with the equipment they need if they should ever find themselves in the situation that Bexleyheath Academy found themselves in on the 5th of February 2013. I have watched Juliet drive a campaign of ensuring that defibrillators are available in all the secondary schools in Bexleyheath.

I have watched Juliet turn her 'ashes into beauty' for the benefit of all those around. I always say to myself that I wish I had met Juliet Lamin under different and much more pleasant circumstances, but as we are always told, '*who are we to question God*?'

Juliet, you are an inspirational and phenomenal woman. I pray God continues to use you as you touch the lives of others and encourage them. I pray that you continue to have the strength to remain tight [sic] when you go through challenging and tough times, and may you continue to see yourself through God's eyes. May the Holy Spirit continue to be with you, comfort you and guide you and may you continue to be highly favoured and blessed – Amen

Lennette

Reflections on Philip Lamin

Philip Lamin, I would say was my 'first nephew.' While cousins of his age called me by name, he had a tender way of calling me

'Auntie Lennette.' This was of course before his voice changed into a 'man's'. Yet when it changed, it still carried a tenderness and respect that I cherished. I remember going to his elementary-primary school to pick him up a couple of times when his Mum, Juliet, asked me to. As young as he was, I could have a conversation with him about anything. Sometimes I'd say, 'you are so young, what do you know?' but he would not allow himself to be so easily dismissed.

Juliet is a powerful woman. The crazy combination of Nigerian-German is already epic; add radical-for-Christ to that and she is a glorious force. The glorious force that she is, Juliet does not leave anyone behind. Not leaving anyone behind means that she would not let me sit at home and pine, lick my wounds or roll around in self-pity when circumstances seemed to have knocked me off my feet. This meant pulling me up to our church building to join her in prayer and intercession. On many of those occasions, Philip 'had to' come with us and I clearly remember the looks of 'I-never-signed-up-for-this' in his eyes. Yet, not once did I ever see him throw a tantrum.

One of my favourite moments with Philip was an African Nations Cup final match between Nigeria and Ghana. Philip's connection to Nigeria surprised me. I had met a number of second generation Brits who had disconnected from their parents' past, so the fact that Philip celebrated Nigeria when he had never been there was surprisingly refreshing. Unfortunately for him that day, my siblings and some friends, who had come over to watch the game, were all supporting Ghana. Philip held his place of conviction and support for Nigeria throughout the whole game. Ghana ended up winning, and poor Philip was teased. He held his ground so strongly, and eventually burst into tears. My dad had to comfort him and talk him into toughening up.

Philip was always so generous to us the 'younger' aunties who wanted to practice our 'not yet parents' parental skills on him. I would stop by the house and he would be on top of his bunk bed, and we'd have a talk about how school was going, and all the basic chitchat. Then I'd scold him on how he should tidy his room, read more and play fewer video games, etc. All he ever said was 'Yes, Auntie. Yes, Auntie.'

I used to think 'Boy, you are a rare breed!'

Since his death, I go back often and read our Facebook messages, which mostly consists of, *'Philip how are you? How is school? Are you home? Where's your Mum? Ask her to pick up her phone*!'

He laughed at my madness so much. It was a bit of a chore trying to be a 'cool' aunt/big sister; telling jokes that made absolutely no sense and watching a young man tolerate me with such generosity.

Philip's death left me with an abstract certainty of the 'Sovereignty of God.' When a sister-friend called me to pray because Philip had collapsed, my first reaction was,

'*Oh Philip, he knows how to keep his mum on her toes. He probably went to play football and was just dehydrated. He'll be fine! This is Philip I'm talking about. This is Juliet I'm talking about. If there is any mother who knows how to sit at the foot of God on behalf of her child, it is Juliet. There's no way God's going to let anything happen to Philip.'*

At that moment, I was reminded of many of the prayers and prophecies that had been prayed over Philip. Many of which I had the privilege of stretching my hands towards or laying my hands on Philip, and joining in agreement with. One particular one that comes to mind was an evening when Juliet, Philip and I happened to have stopped by a fellowship to say hello to some friends. Some Pastors, friends, Juliet, Philip and I formed a circle and took turns putting each person in the centre and praying over each other. I distinctly remember Philip and the words that were spoken over his life. So on February 5, 2013, I would have put my blood on the table to say Philip was going to be fine. I remember hopping on Facebook asking some friends to pray. I started playing, singing and dancing to Ron Kenoly's '*It is such fun to see Satan lose – Jesus is the Winner Man.'* I remember posting that Satan had touched the wrong child because he is sure to lose.

Something sobered me up when I recalled another Pastor who had lost his son at the age of 16. So I took to my room floor, to seek God on behalf of Philip, reiterating all those words of life I had heard spoken over Philip. Two hours later, my Dad called to say, 'He's gone.'

As I stood in the kitchen and heard those words, the truth of the Sovereignty of God descended on me. 'God, you are God indeed. We can pray and cry, but **You** make that final call.'

Philip did not die for lack of prayer. I got on my knees and said, 'Yes, God, Sir, you are the boss! You are Sovereign! Your will be done.' As I was there with my Dad, praying over the phone, another thought descended on me: 'But you can be sure that My Sovereignty is wrapped up in love.'

I was unable to make it back to the UK for Philip's funeral, but every day I was online and on the phone, trying to glean what I could of the impact of this young man's life.

Over the past two years, it is overwhelming to see how every single one of the prophecies I can recall has come to pass in the wake of Philip's death. The countless lives many said Philip would touch, he has touched. His generous, gentle spirit has brought such peace and counsel to the hearts in turmoil from the pain of his loss. When it hurts, remembering his face and voice comes with an indescribable calm.

About 10 days or so after Philip's passing, I was on Facebook, going through his page and suddenly on the chat bar 'Philip Lamin' popped up. My heart skipped as I asked who it was. In the bottom corner, the note appeared '*Philip Lamin is typing....*' For the few seconds it took before the words appeared, I was in a state of shock and fear, as my brain grappled with the thought of Philip, who was no longer here, typing to me. And yes, for a second, I wondered if it was Philip's spirit on Facebook. With bated breath, I waited to find out. It turned out to be a family friend keeping track of messages of consolation on Philip's page. Phew! *Oh Philip, you sure keep us on our toes.*

Natalie Grant's song *Held* is my Philip-Juliet song. As I still try to make sense of what in the world God is doing in this situation, this song speaks out. I finally got to see Juliet in person this past summer, and all I could say was, 'How are you still standing?'

My heart breaks at her pain but I thank her, oh, I thank her with tears streaming down my eyes right now.

Thank you, Juliet, for not giving up on God. Your faith over the years has fuelled so many other people's faith, including mine, and to watch you walk this journey means there is nothing, nothing that life can throw at me that should make me give up.

If Juliet can do it, by God's grace I can too. I remember thinking, *Satan you have truly lost, because if you did not take her out now, ain't nothing more you can do to her.*

I celebrate each day she stands! I look at her and echo: This is what it means to be held, how it feels when the sacred is torn from your life....AND YOU SURVIVE!

'Held' by Natalie Grant[3]

Two months is too little.

They let him go.

They had no sudden healing.

To think that providence would

Take a child from his mother while she prays

Is appalling.

Who told us we'd be rescued?

What has changed and why should we be saved from nightmares?

We're asking why this happens

To us who have died to live?

It's unfair.

Chorus:

This is what it means to be held.

How it feels when the sacred is torn from your

---

3   Held - Songwriter: Wells, Christa Nichole Published by Lyrics © Warner/Chappell Music, Inc., Mike Curb Music

life

And you survive.

This is what it is to be loved.

And to know that the promise was

When everything fell,

We'd be held.

I took Philip for granted and that's the one thing, I'd go back and change. I'd stop to tell him more how much I appreciate his gentle, peaceful, enthusiastic energy. I'd tell him that he is a rare breed. That the impact of his short 16 years is full of power, joy and the narrative of the divine that 61 year-olds cannot match.

Philip lives on.

MIKE

In June 2012, I had the privilege of meeting Juliet Lamin as we talked at Costa Coffee.

Was it fate that our paths crossed at that particular time on that particular date, or was it something much bigger. Neither of us was to know on that day in June, how that moment in time would develop and what challenges were ahead for both of us.

As we got to know each other, Juliet and her son Philip spent some good times with my 3 children and I. Daniel was a year older than Philip and my twins Kieran and Sarah were a year younger.

I knew fairly quickly that Philip felt comfortable with me, as it didn't take him long to contact me directly and ask me to financially sponsor some new clothes and trainers he wanted for meeting Boris Johnson at his school during the Olympics. I remember Juliet was not impressed that he had made such direct requests to me for new trainers.

My relationship with Juliet grew and we were regular visitors to her church in Belvedere. I always had Christian beliefs, but was not a regular churchgoer. It was on Philip's birthday on November 18th 2012 that Juliet first took me to Pastor Del's church. I'm a quiet reserved character and as such was taken by surprise when I became overcome with emotion for no reason I could understand, during the altar call on that day. It was not until later that the significance of me being born again on that day became apparent.

Philip and Juliet spent Christmas 2012 with me and my children. Philip was very competitive, so wasn't best pleased when he was beaten by Sarah at ten pin bowling.

Daniel and Philip shared the same passion for football and both supported Arsenal. My Christmas present to the boys was tickets to watch Arsenal on New Year's Day. It was a shame that it was a 0-0 draw.

As we all spent more time together, Juliet and I got closer and we were all bonding together as a new family. As such, I'll never forget the call I got from Juliet on Tuesday 5th February 2013. I had received a couple of missed calls while driving home, and as I pulled up at home, the phone rang again. I answered and was confronted by a hysterical Juliet saying, 'please tell me Philip will be ok'. I asked where she was and between her requests for me to confirm that Philip would be ok, I was able to establish that Philip had been playing football and now Juliet was at the hospital. I initially thought that he had broken his leg, but as Juliet became more and more incoherent, I asked her to pass the phone to the nurse.

As the nurse answered, I explained that I was Juliet's partner and that I knew Philip was in hospital, I asked her to let me know what happened to Philip. I remember the utter feeling of shock and helplessness when she said the words, 'I'm really sorry to tell you that Philip has passed away.'

I'll never forget feeling so helpless as I was over 2 hours' drive away. As I made my way to the hospital, I just didn't know what to do. I was met at the hospital reception and taken to Juliet by Carol Barefoot, Pastor Del's wife. Juliet sat by herself in the reception area with a massive crowd in a private room close by. I remember the look of bewilderment on her face as I took her in my arms and hugged her.

We went in to see Philip, and as I saw this young fit man lying there, I just felt he looked like he was asleep and would wake up at any moment. Juliet joined in with the prayers over her son as everyone prayed for the miracle that would bring him back to life.

It was clear that nobody wanted to leave Philip's side that night, but soon we all had to make our way out of the hospital, and as I took Juliet back to her house, I remember feeling so numb, but knew I had to be strong for my princess.

I remember the crowds of people that arrived at Juliet's house that night. It was the first time I had met a lot of her friends and well-wishers; as soon as some were ready to leave, more people arrived. There were prayers and tears, but most of all, an outpouring of love and support for Juliet.

The next day Juliet wanted to visit the school. She put on Philip's football shirt and we drove to the school. I remember walking into the school, seeing the faces of staff and pupils as they all dealt with their own grief, not sure what to say to Juliet.

I remember Juliet being so strong that day as she comforted others in their grief.

As I tried to juggle work and being with Juliet over the next few weeks, I remember the daily vigils by her friends at the house. Juliet prayed powerfully every morning, which seemed to give her strength in the public eye, but in private, she would break down as we tried to understand and comprehend why this had happened to her. It was very painful as we had to deal with the fact that the coroner wouldn't give us a timescale to release Philip's body. I remember trying to take much of the necessary phone calls and arrangement-making away from Juliet allowing her to spend her time in prayer, which I could see was helping her in coming to terms with her grief. Throughout this time, I continued to be amazed at the strength she was offering others, particularly Philip's friends and classmates.

We finally got the date when Philip's body was to be released over a month after his passing. Again, at the funeral, I was inspired, as I know so many people were, at Juliet's strength and composure. It was apparent that her strength throughout, but particularly on this day gave other people strength and helped so many come to terms with the grief we were all feeling.

As the weeks and months passed after the funeral the everyday crowds went, but their support continued. I have been so privileged to have been trusted by Juliet to help carry her through this ordeal. We have now passed the second anniversary of Philip's passing, and our relationship has been tested so many times, but the love and trust we have for each other have withstood these tests.

As I witnessed first-hand the strength Juliet got from her faith during these difficult times, I saw how it carried her through day by day, week by week and month by month. She had such a tremendous relationship with God, that has not just allowed her to survive, but has raised her to a new level where she is now an inspiration to so many people, particularly the young people of Bexleyheath. She started PL9 in Philip's memory, which has inspired so many young people locally to develop confident, positive personalities.

It's not just young people that were inspired. I have been, too. Seeing the strength Juliet has got from her faith has encouraged me to want to have such a relationship and receive such spiritual strength. I was inspired to take the next step in developing my relationship with God by being baptised on Easter Sunday 2013.

Whilst Juliet and I often look back with tears when we think about how Philip was taken so young, we are now able to talk about all the positive things that have happened since his passing.

Due to the circumstances of what happened to Juliet during our relationship, and how the strength and encouragement she showed to others has lifted her onto new platforms where she is now able to be an inspiration , my role in the relationship has often been one of quiet support in the background.

I am very proud to be with Juliet, and feel privileged that she loves me so much and trusts me to support her.

I was the happiest man on 24th June 2014, two years to the day that we met, that she accepted my marriage proposal, and I can't wait for us to continue our journey through life together as husband and wife, starting on 12th September 2015.

I love you lots, Juliet

YMUTFE. Xx

My conclusion

12 to 15 healthy young people die every week in the UK alone from cardiac arrest, but there is a 75% chance of survival if a defibrillator is used within five minutes of a child collapsing.

As you read this book, if this touches you in any way and you want to be part of our change to help maximise the chances of cardiac arrest survival in your community, join us. Adopt a school in your local community, set up fundraising activities to raise money and then donate a defibrillator to that school in commemoration of PL9's efforts.

You can get in touch via our website at http://pl9caf.org.uk to see how we can work together. You can also watch the Philip Lamin documentary at:

www.youtube.com/watch?v=DnCzODgi9Ds